Key Concepts in Chinese Thought and Culture

www.royalcollins.com

KEY CONCEPTS IN CHINESE THOUGHT AND CULTURE

I

The editorial board of *Key Concepts in Chinese Thought and Culture*

Books Beyond Boundaries
ROYAL COLLINS

Key Concepts in Chinese Thought and Culture, Volume I

First English Edition 2020
By Royal Collins Publishing Group Inc.
BKM ROYALCOLLINS PUBLISHERS PRIVATE LIMITED
www.royalcollins.com

Headquarters: 550-555 boul. René-Lévesque O Montréal (Québec) H2Z1B1 Canada
India office: 805 Hemkunt House, 8th Floor, Rajendra Place, New Delhi 110 008

ISBN: 978-1-4878-0203-5 (hardcover)
ISBN: 978-1-4878-0220-2 (paperback)

Experts of the Key Concepts in Chinese Thought and Culture-Translation and Communication Project

Academic Board

Foreword

By "key concepts in Chinese thought and culture" we mean concepts and keywords or phrases the Chinese people have created or come to use and that are fundamentally pertinent to Chinese philosophy, humanistic spirit, way of thinking, and values. They represent the Chinese people's exploration of and rational thinking about nature and society over thousands of years. These concepts and expressions reflect the Chinese people's wisdom, their profound spiritual pursuit, as well as the depth and width of their thinking. Their way of thinking, values, and philosophy embodied in these concepts have become a kind of "life gene" in Chinese culture and have long crystallized into the common personality and beliefs of the Chinese nation. For the Chinese people today, they serve as a key to a better understanding of the evolutions of their ancient philosophy, humanistic spirit, way of thinking, and values as well as the development of Chinese literature, art, and history. For people in other countries, these concepts open the door to understanding the spiritual world of contemporary China and the Chinese people, including those living overseas.

In the era of cultural diversity and multipolar discourse today, cultures of different countries and civilizations of different peoples are integrating faster, in greater depth, and on a greater scope than ever before. All countries and peoples have their own systems of thought, culture, and discourse, which should all have their place in the civilization and discourse systems of the world. They all deserve due respect. The concepts in thought and culture of a country and its people are naturally the most essential part of their discourse. They constitute the marrow of a nation's thought, the root of its culture, the soul of its spirit, and the core of its scholarship. More and more people of vision have come to recognize the inspirations Chinese thought and culture might offer to help resolve many difficult problems faced by mankind. The Chinese hold that a man should "have ample virtue and carry all things," "Dao operates naturally," "heaven and man are united as one," a man of virtue seeks "harmony but not uniformity," "people are the foundation of the state," and "study of ancient classics should meet present needs." The Chinese ideals such as "coexistence of all in harmony," "all the people under heaven are one family," and a world of "universal harmony" are drawing increasing attention among the international community. More and more international scholars and friends have become interested in learning and better understanding Chinese thought and culture in general, and the relevant concepts in particular.

In selecting, explaining, translating, and sharing concepts in Chinese thought and culture, we have adopted a comprehensive and systematic approach. Most of them not only reflect the characteristics of Chinese philosophy, humanistic spirit, way of thinking, values, and culture, but also have significance and/or implications that transcend time and national boundaries, and that still fascinate present-day readers and offer them food for thought. It is hoped that the translation of these concepts into English and other languages will help people in other countries to gain a more objective and more rounded understanding of China, of its people, of its past and present, and of the spiritual world of contemporary Chinese. Such understanding should be conducive to promoting equal dialogue between China and other countries and exchanges between different civilizations.

The selection, explanation, and translation of these concepts have been made possible thanks to the support of the Ministry of Education, China International Publishing Group, the Central Compilation and Translation Bureau, Peking University, Renmin University of China, Wuhan University, and Beijing Foreign Studies University, as well as the support of renowned scholars in China and abroad, including Florence Chia-ying Yeh, Li Xueqin, Zhang Qizhi, and Lin Wusun.

The idea of compiling key concepts in Chinese thought and culture represents an innovation and the project calls much research and effort both in connotation and denotation. Furthermore, an endeavor like this has not been previously attempted on such a large scale. Lack of precedents means there must remain much room for improvement. Therefore, we welcome comments from all readers in the hope of better fulfilling this task.

April 11, 2015

Contents

Foreword *vii*

PART I

1 悲慨 bēikǎi
Melancholy and Resentment *3*

2 本末 běnmò
Ben and *Mo* (The Fundamental and the Incidental) *4*

3 般若 bōrě
Buddhist Wisdom *5*

4 不学《诗》，无以言 bù xué shī wú yǐ yán
You Won't Be Able to Talk Properly with Others
Without Studying *The Book of Songs.* *6*

5 诚 chéng
Sincerity *7*

6 大同 dàtóng
Universal Harmony *8*

7 道 dào
Dao (Way) *9*

8 德 dé
De *10*

9 发愤著书 fàfèn-zhùshū
Indignation Spurs One to Write Great Works. 11

10 法治 fǎzhì
Rule by Law 12

11 风雅颂 fēngyǎsòng
Ballad, Court Hymn, and Eulogy 13

12 封建 fēngjiàn
Feudal System / Feudalism 14

13 讽谕 fěngyù
Subtle Admonition 15

14 赋比兴 fùbǐxīng
Narrative, Analogy, and Association 17

15 格调 gédiào
Form and Melody 18

16 华夏 huáxià
Huaxia 19

17 怀远以德 huái yuǎn yǐ dé
Embrace Distant Peoples by Means of Virtue 20

18 肌理 jīlǐ
Reasoning and Structure 21

19 江山 jiāngshān
Rivers and Mountains / Country or State Power 23

20 教化 jiàohuà
Shaping the Mind Through Education 24

21 九州 jiǔzhōu
Nine *Zhou* (Regions) 25

22 科举 kējǔ
The Imperial Civil Examination System 26

23 厉与西施，道通为一 lài yǔ Xīshī, dào tōng wéi yī
A Scabby Person and the Beautiful Lady Xishi Are the Same in the Eyes of Dao. 28

24 乐而不淫，哀而不伤 lè ér bù yín, āi ér bù shāng
Express Enjoyment Without Indulgence and Express Grief Without Excessive Distress 29

25 理 lǐ
Li 30

26 利用厚生 lìyòng-hòushēng
Make Full Use of Resources to Enrich the People 31

27 良史 liángshǐ
Trustworthy Historian / Factual History 32

28 良知 liángzhī
Liangzhi (Conscience) 33

29 六经皆史 liù jīng jiē shǐ
The Six Confucian Classics Are All About History. 34

30 六义 liùyì
The Six Basic Elements 35

31 美刺 měicì
Extolment and Satirical Criticism 37

32 民惟邦本 mín wéi bāng běn
People Being the Foundation of the State 38

33 气 qì
Qi (Vital Force) 39

34 情 qíng
Qing 40

35 情景 qíngjǐng
Sentiment and Scenery 41

36 趣 qù
Qu 42

37 人文化成 rénwén-huàchéng
Ren Wen Hua Cheng 43

38 人治 rénzhì
Rule by Man 44

39 仁 rén
Ren 45

40 日新 rìxīn
Constant Renewal 46

41 镕裁 róngcái
Refining and Deleting 47

42 社稷 shèjì
Sheji (Gods of the Earth and the Five Grains) 48

43 神 shén
Shen (Spirit / Spiritual) 49

44 神思 shénsī
Imaginative Contemplation 50

45 声一无听，物一无文 shēng yī wú tīng, wù yī wú wén
A Single Note Does Not Compose a Melodious Tune,
Nor Does a Single Color Make a Beautiful Pattern. 51

46 圣 shèng
Sage / Sageness 52

47 诗言志 shī yán zhì
Poetry Expresses Aspirations. 53

48 诗缘情 shī yuán qíng
Poetry Springs from Emotions. 54

49 史才三长 shǐ cái sān cháng
Three Strengths of a Good Historian 55

50 书院 shūyuàn
Classical Academy 56

51 顺天应人 shùntiān-yìngrén
Follow the Mandate of Heaven and Comply with the Wishes of the People 58

52 太极 tàijí
Taiji (The Supreme Ultimate) 59

53 太学 tàixué
Imperial Academy 60

54 体性 tǐxìng
Style and Temperament 61

55 体用 tǐyòng
Ti and *Yong* 63

56 天 tiān
Tian (Heaven) 64

57 天下 tiānxià
Tianxia (All Under Heaven) 65

58 王 wáng
King 66

59 王道 wángdào
Kingly Way (Benevolent Governance) 67

60 为政以德 wéi zhèng yǐ dé
Governance Based on Virtue 68

61 文明 wénmíng
Wenming (Civilization) 69

62 文气 wénqì
Wenxqi *70*

63 文以载道 wén yǐ zài dào
Literature Is the Vehicle of Ideas. *71*

64 无为 wúwéi
Non-action *72*

65 五行 wǔxíng
Wuxing *73*

66 物 wù
Wu (Thing / Matter) *74*

67 象外之象，景外之景 xiàng wài zhī xiàng, jǐng wài zhī jǐng
The Image Beyond an Image, the Scene Beyond a Scene *75*

68 协和万邦 xiéhé-wànbāng
Coexistence of All in Harmony *76*

69 心 xīn
Heart / Mind *77*

70 信言不美，美言不信 xìn yán bù měi, měi yán bù xìn
Trustworthy Words May Not Be Fine-sounding;
Fine-sounding Words May Not Be Trustworthy. *78*

71 兴观群怨 xīngguānqúnyuàn
Stimulation, Contemplation, Communication, and Criticism *79*

72 兴象 xīngxiàng
Xingxiang (Inspiring Imagery) *81*

73 性 xìng
Xing (Nature) *82*

74 性灵 xìnglíng
Xingling (Inner Self) *83*

75 修齐治平 xiūqízhìpíng
Self-cultivation, Family Regulation, State Governance, Bringing Peace to All Under Heaven 85

76 虚 xū
Xu 86

77 虚静 xūjìng
Void and Peace 87

78 玄览 xuánlǎn
Xuanlan (Pure-minded Contemplation) 88

79 选举 xuǎnjǔ
Select and Recommend 89

80 雅俗 yǎsú
Highbrow and Lowbrow 90

81 养气 yǎngqì
Cultivating *Qi* 91

82 一 yī
The One 92

83 义 yì
Righteousness 93

84 意象 yìxiàng
Yixiang (Imagery) 94

85 阴阳 yīnyáng
Yin and Yang 95

86 隐秀 yǐnxiù
Latent Sentiment and Evident Beauty 96

87 有德者必有言 yǒu dé zhě bì yǒu yán
Virtuous People Are Sure to Produce Fine Writing. 97

88 有教无类 yǒujiào-wúlèi
Education for All Without Discrimination 98

89 有无 yǒuwú
You and *Wu* 99

90 缘起 yuánqǐ
Dependent Origination 100

91 知音 zhīyīn
Resonance and Empathy 101

92 直寻 zhíxún
Direct Quest 102

93 中国 zhōngguó
Zhongguo (China) 103

94 中华 zhōnghuá
Zhonghua 104

95 中庸 zhōngyōng
Zhongyong (Golden Mean) 105

96 滋味 zīwèi
Nuanced Flavor 106

97 紫之夺朱 zǐ zhī duó zhū
Purple Prevailing over Red 107

98 自然 zìrán
Naturalness 108

99 自然英旨 zìrán yīngzhǐ
Charm of Spontaneity 109

100 宗法 zōngfǎ
Feudal Clan System 111

PART II

101 安土重迁 āntǔ-zhòngqiān
Attached to the Land and Unwilling to Move 115

102 八卦 bāguà
Eight Trigrams 116

103 本色 běnsè
Bense (Original Character) 117

104 比德 bǐdé
Virtue Comparison 119

105 辨体 biàntǐ
Style Differentiation 120

106 别材别趣 biécái-biéqù
Distinct Subject and Artistic Taste 122

107 别集 biéjí
Individual Collection 124

108 城 chéng
Fortress / City 126

109 楚辞 chǔcí
Chuci (Ode of Chu) 127

110 唇亡齿寒 chúnwáng-chǐhán
Once the Lips Are Gone, the Teeth Will Feel Cold. 129

111 辞达 cídá
Expressiveness 130

112 道法自然 dào fǎ zìrán
Dao Operates Naturally. 131

113 都 dū
Metropolis 132

114 独化 dúhuà
Self-driven Development 133

115 法不阿贵 fǎ bù ē guì
The Law Does Not Favor the Rich and Powerful. 134

116 非攻 fēigōng
Denouncing Unjust Wars 135

117 干城 gānchéng
Shield and Fortress / Dukes and Princes 136

118 刚柔 gāngróu
Gang and *Rou* 137

119 革命 gémìng
Changing the Mandate / Revolution 138

120 格物致知 géwù-zhìzhī
Study Things to Acquire Knowledge 139

121 卦爻 guàyáo
Trigrams and Component Lines 140

122 国家 guójiā
Family-state / Country 141

123 国体 guótǐ
Guoti 142

124 过犹不及 guòyóubùjí
Going Too Far Is as Bad as Falling Short. 143

125 海内 hǎinèi
Within the Four Seas 144

126 海外 hǎiwài
Outside the Four Seas / Overseas 145

127 和而不同 hé' érbùtóng
Harmony But Not Uniformity 146

128 厚德载物 hòudé-zàiwù
Have Ample Virtue and Carry All Things 147

129 化干戈为玉帛 huà gāngē wéi yùbó
Beat Swords into Plowshares / Turn War into Peace 148

130 化工、画工 huàgōng, huàgōng
Magically Natural, Overly Crafted 149

131 画道 huàdào
Dao of Painting 150

132 画龙点睛 huàlóng-diǎnjīng
Adding Pupils to the Eyes of a Painted Dragon / Rendering the Final Touch 151

133 会心 huìxīn
Heart-to-heart Communication 152

134 浑沌 hùndùn
Chaos 153

135 活法 huófǎ
Literary Flexibility 154

136 兼爱 jiān'ài
Universal Love 156

137 解衣盘礴 jiěyī-pánbó
Sitting with Clothes Unbuttoned and Legs Stretching Out 157

138 京(京师) jīng (jīngshī)
Capital of a Country 159

139 经济 jīngjì
To Govern and Help the People 160

140 经世致用 jīngshì-zhìyòng
Study of Ancient Classics Should Meet Present Needs. 162

141 境界 jìngjiè
Jingjie (Visionary World) 164

142 境生象外 jìng shēng xiàng wài
Aesthetic Conception Transcends Concrete Objects Described. 166

143 居安思危 jū'ān-sīwēi
Be on Alert Against Potential Danger When Living in Peace 168

144 君 jūn
Lord / Nobility / Monarch 169

145 君子 jūnzǐ
Junzi (Man of Virtue) 170

146 开物成务 kāiwù-chéngwù
Understand Things and Succeed in One's Endeavors 171

147 坤 kūn
Kun 172

148 礼 lǐ
Li (Rites / Social Norms) 173

149 妙悟 miàowù
Subtle Insight 174

150 民胞物与 mínbāo-wùyǔ
All People Are My Brothers and Sisters,
and All Things Are My Companions. 176

151 名实 míngshí
Name and Substance 177

152 命 mìng
Mandate / Destiny 178

153 气象 qìxiàng
Prevailing Features 179

154 乾 qián
Qian 181

155 取境 qǔjìng
Qujing (Conceptualize an Aestheric Feeling) 182

156 人道 réndào
Way of Man 183

157 人文 rénwén
Renwen 184

158 三玄 sānxuán
Three Metaphysical Classics 185

159 上帝 shàngdì
Supreme Ruler / Ruler of Heaven 186

160 上善若水 shàngshànruòshuǐ
Great Virtue Is Like Water. 187

161 神与物游 shén yǔ wù yóu
Interaction Between the Mind and the Subject Matter 188

162 神韵 shényùn
Elegant Subtlety 190

163 师出有名 shīchū-yǒumíng
Fighting a War with a Moral Justification 192

164 诗史 shīshǐ
Historical Poetry 193

165 诗中有画，画中有诗 shī zhōng yǒu huà, huà zhōng yǒu shī
Painting in Poetry, Poetry in Painting 194

166 实事求是 shíshì-qiúshì
Seek Truth from Facts 195

167 思 sī
Reflecting / Thinking 196

168 斯文 sīwén
Be Cultured and Refined 197

169 四端 sìduān
Four Initiators 198

170 四海 sìhǎi
Four Seas 199

171 四书 sìshū
Four Books 200

172 体 tǐ
Ti 201

173 天人合一 tiānrén-héyī
Heaven and Man Are United as One. 203

174 天人之分 tiānrénzhīfēn
Distinction Between Man and Heaven 204

175 天子 tiānzǐ
Son of Heaven 205

176 温柔敦厚 wēnróu-dūnhòu
Mild, Gentle, Sincere, and Broadminded 206

177 文笔 wénbǐ
Writing and Writing Technique 207

178 文学 wénxué
Literature 209

179 文章 wénzhāng
Literary Writing 211

180 吴越同舟 Wú-Yuè-tóngzhōu
People of Wu and Yue Are in the Same Boat. 213

181 五经 wǔjīng
Five Classics 214

182 逍遥 xiāoyáo
Carefree *215*

183 小人 xiǎorén
Petty Man *216*

184 兴寄 xīngjì
Xingji (Association and Inner Sustenance) *217*

185 兴趣 xīngqù
Xingqu (Charm) *219*

186 形而上 xíng'érshàng
What Is Above Form / The Metaphysical *220*

187 形而下 xíng'érxià
What Is Under Form / The Physical *221*

188 虚壹而静 xūyī'érjìng
Open-mindedness, Concentration, and Tranquility *222*

189 学 xué
Learn *223*

190 养民 yǎngmín
Nurturing the People *224*

191 艺术 yìshù
Art *225*

192 意境 yìjìng
Aesthetic Conception *227*

193 意兴 yìxīng
Inspirational Appreciation *229*

194 宇宙 yǔzhòu
Universe / Cosmos *230*

195 元 yuán
Yuan (Origin) *231*

196 政治 zhèngzhì
Decree and Governance / Politics 232

197 知行 zhīxíng
Knowledge and Application 233

198 止戈为武 zhǐgēwéiwǔ
Stopping War Is a True Craft of War. 234

199 自强不息 zìqiáng-bùxī
Striving Continuously to Strengthen Oneself 235

200 总集 zǒngjí
General Collection / Anthology 236

PART III

201 白描 báimiáo
Plain Line Drawing 241

202 变化 biànhuà
Change 243

203 沉郁 chényù
Melancholy 244

204 诚意 chéngyì
Be Sincere in Thought 245

205 春秋 chūnqiū
The Spring and Autumn Annals / The Spring and Autumn Period 246

206 词 cí
Ci (Lyric) 248

207 词曲 cíqǔ
Ci (Lyric) and *Qu* (Melody) 250

208 错彩镂金 cuòcǎi-lòujīn
Gilded and Colored, Elegant and Refined 251

209 大道至简 dàdào-zhìjiǎn
Great Truth in Simple Words 252

210 大巧若拙 dàqiǎo-ruòzhuō
Exquisite Skill Looks Simple and Clumsy. 254

211 大体、小体 dàtǐ, xiǎotǐ
The Major Organ and the Minor Organs 255

212 大用 dàyòng
Maximal Functioning 256

213 丹青 dānqīng
Painting in Colors 257

214 淡泊 dànbó
Quiet Living with No Worldly Desire 258

215 淡泊明志，宁静致远 dànbó-míngzhì, níngjìng-zhìyuǎn
Indifference to Fame and Fortune Characterizes a High Aim in Life, and Leading a Quiet Life Helps One Accomplish Something Lasting. 259

216 当行 dāngháng
Professionalism 260

217 道济天下 dàojìtiānxià
Support All People by Upholding Truth and Justice 261

218 得道多助，失道寡助 dédào-duōzhù, shīdào-guǎzhù
A Just Cause Enjoys Abundant Support While an Unjust Cause Finds Little Support. 263

219 德性之知 déxìngzhīzhī
Knowledge from One's Moral Nature 265

220 典雅 diǎnyǎ
Classical Elegance 266

221 鼎 dǐng
Ding (Vessel) 267

222 动静 dòngjìng
Movement and Stillness 268

223 多行不义必自毙 duō xíng bù yì bì zì bì
He Who Repeatedly Commits Wrongdoing Will Come to No Good End. 269

224 繁缛 fánrù
Overly Elaborative 270

225 风骨 fēnggǔ
Fenggu 271

226 风教 fēngjiào
Moral Cultivation 273

227 芙蓉出水 fúróng-chūshuǐ
Lotus Rising Out of Water 275

228 刚柔相济 gāngróu-xiāngjì
Combine Toughness with Softness 276

229 歌 gē
Song 277

230 革故鼎新 gégù-dǐngxīn
Do Away with the Old and Set Up the New 278

231 公生明，廉生威 gōng shēng míng, lián shēng wēi
Fairness Fosters Discernment and Integrity Creates Authority. 279

232 浩然之气 hàoránzhīqì
Noble Spirit 280

233 寄托 jìtuō
Entrusting 281

234 见利思义 jiànlì-sīyì
Think of Righteousness in the Face of Gain 282

235 见闻之知 jiànwénzhīzhī
Knowledge from One's Senses 283

236 见贤思齐 jiànxián-sīqí
When Seeing a Person of High Caliber, Strive to Be His Equal. 284

237 鉴古知今 jiàngǔ-zhījīn
Review the Past to Understand the Present 285

238 尽心 jìnxīn
Exert One's Heart / Mind to the Utmost 287

239 空灵 kōnglíng
Ethereal Effect 288

240 旷达 kuàngdá
Broad-mindedness / Unconstrained Style 290

241 礼尚往来 lǐshàngwǎnglái
Reciprocity as a Social Norm 292

242 理一分殊 lǐyī-fēnshū
There Is But One *Li* (Universal Principle),
Which Exists in Diverse Forms. 293

243 内美 nèiměi
Inner Beauty 294

244 否极泰来 pǐjí-tàilái
When Worse Comes to the Worst,
Things Will Turn for the Better. 295

245 飘逸 piāoyì
Natural Grace 296

246 齐物 qíwù
Seeing Things as Equal 297

247 器 qì
Qi (Vessel) 298

248 气骨 qìgǔ
Qigu (Emotional Vitality and Forcefulness) 299

249 气质之性 qìzhìzhīxìng
Character Endowed by *Qi* (Vital Force) 300

250 前事不忘，后事之师 qiánshì-bùwàng, hòushìzhīshī
Past Experience, If Not Forgotten, Is a Guide for the Future. 301

251 求放心 qiú fàngxīn
Search for the Lost Heart 302

252 曲 qǔ
Qu (Melody) 303

253 仁者爱人 rénzhě'àirén
The Benevolent Person Loves Others. 305

254 三表 sānbiǎo
Three Standards 306

255 三才 sāncái
The Three Elements 307

256 三思而行 sānsī'érxíng
Think Thrice Before Acting 308

257 慎独 shèndú
Shendu 309

258 慎思明辨 shènsī-míngbiàn
Careful Reflection and Clear Discrimination 310

259 诗 shī
Shi (Poetry) 311

260 师直为壮 shīzhí-wéizhuàng
Troops Will Be Powerful When Fighting a Just Cause. 313

261 授人以渔 shòurényǐyú
Teaching How to Fish 314

262 恕 shù
Being Considerate / Forgiveness 315

263 四海之内皆兄弟 sì hǎi zhī nèi jiē xiōng dì
All the People Within the Four Seas Are Brothers. 316

264 太虚 tàixū
Taixu (Great Void) 317

265 天道 tiāndào
Way of Heaven 318

266 天理 tiānlǐ
Natural Law 320

267 天命 tiānmìng
Mandate of Heaven 321

268 天命之性 tiānmìngzhīxìng
Character Endowed by Heaven 322

269 天下兴亡，匹夫有责 tiānxià-xīngwáng, pǐfū-yǒuzé
The Rise and Fall of All Under Heaven Is the Responsibility of Every Individual. 323

270 同归殊途 tóngguī-shūtú
Arrive at the Same Destination via Different Routes / Rely on a Common Ontological Entity 325

271 温故知新 wēngù-zhīxīn
Review the Old and Learn the New 326

272 无欲则刚 wúyù-zégāng
People with No Covetous Desires Stand Upright. 327

273 相反相成 xiāngfǎn-xiāngchéng
Being both Opposite and Complementary 328

274 象 xiàng
Xiang (Semblance) 329

275 小说 xiǎoshuō
Fiction 331

276 写意 xiěyì
Freehand Brushwork 333

277 心知 xīnzhī
Mind Cognition 335

278 行先知后 xíngxiān-zhīhòu
First Action, Then Knowledge 336

279 玄 xuán
Xuan (Mystery) 337

280 血气 xuèqì
Vitality / Vital Force 338

281 循名责实 xúnmíng-zéshí
Hold Actualities According to Its Name 339

282 雅乐 yǎyuè
Fine Music 340

283 言不尽意 yánbùjìnyì
Words Cannot Fully Express Thought. 342

284 言尽意 yánjìnyì
Words Can Fully Express Thought. 343

285 炎黄 Yán-Huáng
The Fiery Emperor and the Yellow Emperor /
Emperor Yan and Emperor Huang 344

286 一物两体 yīwù-liǎngtǐ
One Thing in Two Fundamental States 346

287 以无为本 yǐwú-wéiběn
Wu Is the Origin. 347

288 以直报怨 yǐzhí-bàoyuàn
Repaying a Grudge with Rectitude 348

289 有容乃大 yǒuróng-nǎidà
A Broad Mind Achieves Greatness. 349

290 与民更始 yǔmín-gēngshǐ
Make a Fresh Start with the People 350

291 载舟覆舟 zàizhōu-fùzhōu
Carry or Overturn the Boat / Make or Break 351

292 正名 zhèngmíng
Rectification of Names 352

293 正心 zhèngxīn
Rectify One's Heart / Mind 353

294 政者正也 zhèng zhě zhèng yě
Governance Means Rectitude. 354

295 知耻而后勇 zhī chǐ ér hòu yǒng
Having a Feeling of Shame Gives Rise to Courage. 355

296 知行合一 zhīxíng-héyī
Unity of Knowledge and Action 356

297 知先行后 zhīxiān-xínghòu
First Knowledge, Then Action 357

298 直 zhí
Rectitude 358

299 治大国若烹小鲜 zhì dà guó ruò pēng xiǎo xiān
Governing a Big Country Is Like Cooking Small Fish. 359

300 忠 zhōng
Loyalty 360

A Brief Chronology of Chinese History 361

PART I

1

bēikǎi
悲慨

Melancholy and Resentment

Melancholy and resentment, which here refers to a sense of helplessness found in poems, is one of the 24 poetic styles summarized by Sikong Tu, a poet in the late Tang Dynasty. Faced with frustrations and tough challenges in life, or overwhelmed by the immensity of nature or major events, poets were often seized by dejection, grief, sadness, and anger, which gave rise to a "melancholy and resentment" style in poetry writing. While the style bears similarity with the genre of tragedy in Western literary tradition, it is more influenced by Daoism, often featuring a sense of resignation or stoic optimism.

CITATIONS

Winds are howling, waves raging, and tree branches breaking. Gripped by an agonizing pain at my heart, I yearn for a spell of peace but only in vain. As time slips by, year after year, decade after decade, all the riches, fame, and splendor are but nothing. Facing moral degeneration, who will rise and salvage the world? With sword in hand, I heave a deep sigh and stare intensely at the sky. Overwhelmed with sorrow, all I can do is to watch leaves falling and hear rain beating against the moss. (Sikong Tu: Twenty-four Styles of Poetry)

After a deep sigh, he wrote a poem to admonish and comfort me, in which he expressed his indignation and resentment by making an analogy with imagery. He advised me not to grudge about tough times or be complacent when everything goes well in life. (Su Shi: A Poem in Reply to Wang Jinqing with a Preface)

2

bĕnmò

本末

Ben and *Mo* (The Fundamental and the Incidental)

The two characters literally mean the different parts of a plant, namely, its root and its foliage. The extended meaning is an important concept in Chinese philosophical discourse. The term can be understood in three different ways. 1) *Ben* (本) refers to what is fundamental or essential, while *mo* (末) means what is minor or incidental, two qualities that differ in value and importance. 2) *Ben* refers to the existence of the world in an ontological sense, while *mo* represents any specific thing or phenomenon. 3) In Daoist political philosophy *ben* is a state in which rule is exercised by not disrupting the natural order of the world, while *mo* refers to moral standards and fundamental principles governing social behavior. In any *ben-mo* relationship, *ben* is most important and plays a dominant role, while *mo* exists thanks to *ben*. On the other hand, it is through the vehicle of *mo* that *ben* exerts its influence. Thus the two, though different, are mutually dependent.

CITATIONS

Zixia's students can clean, receive guests, and engage in social interaction, but these are trivial things. They have not learned the fundamentals. How can this be sufficient? (*The Analects*)

One should respect, not interfere with, the natural order of the world, and apply this principle when establishing moral standards, social norms, and laws and regulations. (Wang Bi: *Commentaries on Laozi*)

3

bōrě
般若

Buddhist Wisdom

The term is the transliteration of the Sanskrit word *prajñā,* meaning wisdom. It refers to the supreme wisdom with insight into the nature and reality of all things. Buddhism believes that such wisdom surpasses all secular understandings, and therefore is the guide for or essence of the effort aimed at achieving enlightenment and attaining Buddhahood or bodhisattvahood. This wisdom has no form, no appearance, and cannot be expressed in words. It can only be achieved by undertaking a variety of accessible Buddhist practices.

CITATION

Prajñā is the wisdom that surpasses all common or ordinary knowledge and specific understandings. (Sengzhao: *Treatises of Sengzhao*)

4

bù xué shī, wú yǐ yán

不学《诗》，无以言

You Won't Be Able to Talk Properly with Others Without Studying *The Book of Songs*.

In Confucius' time, how well one understood *The Book of Songs* was a sign of his social status and cultural attainment. If one did not study it, one would find it difficult to improve one's ability to express oneself and to converse with people of high social status. Confucius' elaboration on the relationship between studying *The Book of Songs* and social interaction actually expounds on the importance of literature in education.

CITATION

Confucius was standing alone in the central hall when his son Boyu walked across the front yard. Confucius asked, "Have you studied *The Book of Songs*?" "Not yet," was the reply. Confucius then said, "If you do not study it, you will not be able to express yourself properly." (*The Analects*)

5

chéng

诚

Sincerity

Sincerity is among the core concepts of the Confucian school of thought. Basically, it means truthfulness without deceit. Confucians believed that sincerity is the essence of the "way of heaven" or "principles of heaven," a basis on which everything else is built. At the same time, sincerity is also the root and foundation of morality. All moral deeds must be conducted on the basis of sincerity from the bottom of the heart. Otherwise, they are nothing but pretensions. *The Doctrine of the Mean* maintains, "Nothing can be achieved without sincerity." Sages are sincere by nature. Therefore, their words and deeds are naturally consistent with the "way of heaven" and the "principles of heaven." *Junzi* (a man of virtue) upholds sincerity as his goal for moral attainment and an approach to achieving the "way of heaven" and the "principles of heaven."

CITATIONS

Being as it is is the way of nature; being true to human nature is the way to achieve self-refinement. (*The Book of Rites*)

Sincerity means utter truthfulness without any pretensions or deceit. It is the natural state of the principles of heaven. (Zhu Xi: *Annotations on The Doctrine of the Mean*)

6

dàtóng

大同

Universal Harmony

This term refers to the time of peace and prosperity envisioned by Confucian scholars when all the people under heaven are one family, equal, friendly, and helpful to each other (as opposed to *xiaokang* [小康] – minor or moderate prosperity). Confucianism takes universal harmony as the supreme stage of the development of the human society, somewhat similar to the idea of utopia in the West. Its main features are: All power and wealth belong to the whole of society; all people are equal and live and work in peace and contentment; everyone is cared for by society; everything is used to its fullest and everyone works to his maximum potential. In the late Qing Dynasty and the early Republic of China, the term referred to the concepts of socialism, communism, or cosmopolitanism that had been introduced to China from the West.

CITATION

When great Dao prevails, the whole world is owned by all the people. Those who are virtuous and competent are selected as administrators. People treat each other with sincerity and live in harmony. People not only love their parents, bring up their children, but also take care of the aged. The middle-aged are able to put their talents and abilities to best use, children are well nurtured, and old widows and widowers, unmarried old people, orphans, childless old people, and the disabled are all provided for… This is universal harmony. (*The Book of Rites*)

7

dào
道

Dao (Way)

In its original meaning, *dao* (道) is the way or path taken by people. It has three extended meanings: 1) the general laws followed by things in different spheres, e.g. the natural order by which the sun, moon and stars move is called the way of heaven; the rules that govern human activities are the way of man; 2) the universal patterns followed by all things and beings; and 3) the original source or ontological existence of things, which transcends form and constitutes the basis for the birth and existence of all things, and for the activities of human beings. In their respective discussions of Dao, Confucianism, Daoism, and Buddhism imbue it with ver y different connotations. While benevolence, righteousness, social norms, and music education form the basic content of the Confucian Dao, the Buddhist and Daoist Dao tends to emphasize *kong* (空 emptiness) and *wu* (无 void).

CITATIONS

The way of heaven is far away; the way of man is near. (*Zuo's Commentary on The Spring and Autumn Annals*)

What transcends form is called Dao. (*The Book of Changes*)

8

dé
德

De

The term has two different meanings. One is an individual's fine moral character, or his proper conduct in society. At first *de* (德) was only related to an individual's behavior, referring to his external moral conduct. Later, it also referred to something that combined external behavior with internal emotions and moral consciousness. The other meaning of *de* refers to the special laws and features obtained from Dao, or the physical manifestation of the hidden and formless Dao, as well as the internal basis for the origination and existence of all things.

CITATIONS

Heaven gives birth to people, provides them with goods and materials, and subjects them to rules. People obey universal rules and value virtues. (*The Book of Songs*)

Dao creates all things under heaven while *de* nurtures them. (*Laozi*)

9

fàfèn-zhùshū

发愤著书

Indignation Spurs One to Write Great Works.

This term means suffering injustice in life can spur one to create great works. It originated from the "Preface by the Grand Historian to *Records of the Historian*." After Sima Qian, an official in the Western Han Dynasty, suffered the unjust punishment of castration, his indignation spurred him to write the great work, *Records of the Historian*. In the book he gave expression to his thoughts, feelings, and aspirations, which made the book a classic for later generations. The expression "indignation spurs one to write great works" was used to explain one of the motivations and reasons for creating masterpieces. It points to the fact that injustice suffered by an author often turns out to be the source of inspiration for him to write a literary masterpiece. It later led to similar terms like "Where there is injustice there will be an expression of indignation" and "Frustration inspires poets to write fine poems."

CITATIONS

I am saddened that my frank remonstration with the king has brought false accusations on me and left me in exile. In anguish and indignation, I am writing these poems to express my strong feelings. (Qu Yuan: *Collection of Nine Pieces*)

Most of the 300 poems in *The Book of Songs* were written by sages who were in anguish and indignation. They were depressed over what had prevented them from fulfilling their aspirations, so they composed poems about what had happened in the hope that future generations would understand them. (Sima Qian: A Letter of Reply to Ren An)

10

fǎzhì

法治

Rule by Law

Rule by law, as opposed to rule by man, calls for ruling a state and its people by the ruler through enacting and strictly enforcing laws and regulations. It is an important political thought of the Legalist scholars in the pre-Qin period. Rule by law meted out well-defined rewards and punishments, but tended to be excessively severe and rigid in enforcement. From the Han Dynasty all the way to the Qing Dynasty, rule by law and rule by man were exercised by various dynasties, mostly in combination. With the spread of Western thoughts to China in more recent times, rule by law acquired new meanings.

CITATIONS

When our forefathers ruled the state, they did not act unscrupulously in disregard of law, nor did they bestow personal favors within the framework of law. (*Guanzi*)

Therefore, rule by law is the supreme way to rule a country. It has been exercised by numerous countries in the world for several thousand years. Who conceived this idea and developed it into a theory of governance? It was none other than our fellow countryman Guanzi! (Liang Qichao: *A Critical Biography of Guanzi*)

11

fēngyǎsòng
风雅颂

Ballad, Court Hymn, and Eulogy

In *The Book of Songs*, the content is divided into three categories according to style and tune: *feng* (ballad), *ya* (court hymn), and *song* (eulogy). Ballads are music from different regions, mostly folk songs. Court hymns, divided into *daya* (major hymn) and *xiaoya* (minor hymn), are songs sung at court banquets or grand ceremonies. They are mostly the works by lettered noblemen. Eulogies are ritual or sacrificial dance music and songs, most of which praise the achievements of ancestors. Court hymns and eulogies are highbrow songs while ballads are lowbrow ones. Therefore, ballads, court hymns, and eulogies not only refer to the styles of *The Book of Songs* but also classify the songs into highbrow and lowbrow categories. Later on *fengya* (风雅) generally referred to anything elegant.

CITATIONS

Therefore *The Book of Songs* has six basic elements: ballads, narratives, analogies, associations, court hymns, and eulogies. (Preface to *The Book of Songs*)

The three "longitudes" of *The Book of Songs* refer to narrative, analogy, and association, which serve as the frame of a poem. Without these, they could not be called poems. If narrative is not used in a poem, analogy must be used; if analogy is not used, association must be employed. Ballads from the states, court hymns, and eulogies play a connecting role in the poems. Since the poems have narrative, analogy, and association serving as the "longitudes," ballads from the states, court hymns, and eulogies are therefore called the three "latitudes." (*Classified Conversations of Master Zhu Xi*)

12

fēngjiàn

封建

Feudal System / Feudalism

In feudalism, the lord granted titles of nobility, fiefs, and people to his relatives and officials and allowed them to establish dukedoms. A fief was smaller than the territory under the direct control of the lord. While obeying the rule of the lord, a dukedom enjoyed a high degree of autonomy in its military and administrative affairs. Dukedoms checked each other in the protection of the lord. A dukedom might be passed down genetically upon the approval of the lord and was required to pay tribute to him. As a political system, feudalism is believed to have started in the era of the legendary Yellow Emperor, and became established in the Western Zhou Dynasty. Feudalism was akin to the patriarchal clan system based on blood ties and gave rise to a hierarchy system. After Qinshihuang, the first emperor of Qin, reunified China, he abolished feudalism in favor of the system of prefectures and counties. From the Qin Dynasty to the Qing Dynasty, centralized government or imperial autocracy was dominant in China, rendering feudalism, which existed overtly or covertly, supplementary.

CITATION

Feudal system survived the eras of all ancient sages, namely Yao, Shun, Yu the Great, Tang of Shang, King Wen of Zhou, and King Wu of Zhou. (Liu Zongyuan: *On Feudal System*)

13

fěngyù
讽谕

Subtle Admonition

The term refers to the use of allegories to convey popular mood and public opinion and make critical comments on state affairs to the ruler in a tactful manner in the hope to persuade him to correct wrong policies. *Feng* (讽) represents making critical but persuasive comments subtly through poetry or prose; *yu* (喻) means delivering an explicit message. Such literary writing is intended to be both critical and persuasive; and it has two integral aspects, namely, a subtle literary way of expression as required by *feng*, and its social function of sending explicit messages to the ruler as required. The theory of subtle admonition was advocated by scholars of the Han Dynasty based on their interpretation of *The Book of Songs*. Confucian scholars from then on promoted the use of subtle admonition to influence decision-making of the ruler and social mores in a literary way. Bai Juyi, a poet of the Tang Dynasty, wrote many such poems, further reinforcing the social function of poetry and advancing this literary tradition, which had great impact on literary creation of later generations.

CITATIONS

Some literary works use subtle admonition to convey what the subjects think and feel, in the hope that the subtle advice could reach the ruler, whereas other works expound the kindness and benevolence of the ruler so as to guide the populace to fulfilling their duties and obligations. (Ban Gu: Preface to "Essays on Chang'an and Luoyang")

Writings by ancient scholars could be said that at a higher level they aimed at explaining some kind of link between the ideas of the ruling court and popular sentiment in society. At a more practical level, they sent a clear message of advice to the rulers through allegories. (Bai Juyi: *Collection of Essays in Preparation for the Final Round of the Imperial Exam*)

14

fùbǐxīng
赋比兴

Narrative, Analogy, and Association

These are the three ways of expression employed in *The Book of S ongs*: a narrative is a direct reference t o an object or an event, an analogy metaphorically likens one thing to another, and an association is an impromptu expression of a feeling, a mood or a thought, or using an objective thing as metaphor for sensibilities. Confucian scholars of the Han Dynasty summarized and formulated this concept of narrative, analogy, and association, which later became the basic principle and method in classical Chinese literary creation.

CITATIONS

In *The Book of Songs*, narrative, analogy, and association are three techniques in its creation, whereas ballads, court hymns, and eulogies represent three established styles of the poems. (Kong Yingda: Correct Meaning of "Preface to *The Book of Songs*")

A narrative is a direct description of an object, an event or a relationship. An analogy metaphorically likens one thing to another. An association employs a metaphor as a lead-in for the real subject of a poem. (Zhu Xi: *Studies on The Book of Songs*)

15

gédiào
格调

Form and Melody

The term refers to the form and metrical patterns, as well as content, of poetry. It relates to artistic taste and appeal in poetry criticism. *Ge* (格) refers to the need to satisfy established metrical rules, while *diao* (调) refers to the need to follow tone and rhyme schemes in poetry. Some poetry critics of the Tang and Song dynasties stressed the importance of form and melody in order to establish a set of elegant and authoritative standards for poetry. Theory on form and melody in the Ming and Qing dynasties often emphasized the importance for poets to abide by Confucian orthodoxy, thus constraining their expression of feelings and artistic creations. The term was later also used in discussions of other forms of art.

CITATIONS

To be elegant and unaffected is to satisfy the requirements of form; to be tuneful and resonant is to follow the rules of melody. (Li Mengyang: *Arguments Against He Jingming's Views*)

Jiang Kui's poems are characterized by ethereal purity. Though tinged with loneliness and sadness at times, they are of high standard and taste. (Chen Tingzhuo: *Remarks on Lyrics from White Rain Studio*)

16

huáxià

华夏

Huaxia

The forefathers of the Han people living in the Central Plains referred to themselves by this term. Earlier on they called themselves Hua (华), Zhuhua (诸华), Xia (夏) or Zhuxia (诸夏). The term Huaxia (华夏) embodies the common identity of the way of life, language, and culture of the people living in the Central Plains, mainly the Han people, and the inheritance of such identity. The Huaxia people evolved into a fairly stable ethnic group in the Qin Dynasty, which established a unified country of many ethnic groups with Huaxia being the principal group. In the Han Dynasty, the term Han became an alternative name of Huaxia. Later, the term Huaxia was extended to refer to China or the Han people.

CITATION

The Chinese character 夏 (*xia*) means big and great. Since the ancient Huaxia people practiced grand and elaborate rituals, they called themselves Xia (great). Their dresses were resplendent, so they were referred to as Hua (splendid). Therefore, both Hua and Xia refer to the Han people. (Kong Yingda: *Correct Meaning of Zuo's Commentary on The Spring and Autumn Annals*)

17

huái yuǎn yǐ dé

怀远以德

Embrace Distant Peoples by Means of Virtue

This expression refers to pursuing conciliatory and benevolent policies and offering benefits to tribes and groups in remote areas. It was a political concept adopted by successive governments led mostly by the Han people in their relations with other ethnic groups, tribes in remote areas not yet directly under their rule, and foreign states. It also represented an important component of the theory of winning over others by virtue. China was, as it is today, a multi-ethnic country. The Han-led government ruled over a large territory and believed that they had an advanced culture. They usually took a conciliatory approach based on the Confucian concept of benevolence in dealing with the tribes and populations in remote regions, rather than conquering them by force, with the goal of placating them and winning their allegiance.

CITATION

Guan Zhong said to the Marquis of Qi, "I have heard it said: Win over the disaffected with respect and embrace distant peoples with virtue. With virtue and respect unchanging, there is no one that will not be embraced." (*Zuo's Commentary on The Spring and Autumn Annals*)

18

jīlǐ

肌理

Reasoning and Structure

The term originally refers to the texture of muscle, and later by extension it refers to well-organized principles in things. As a literary term, it was first used by Weng Fanggang, a Qing-dynasty scholar, to refer to two aspects: *yili* (义理 reasoning) and *wenli* (文理 structure). The former is about views or reasoning, primarily concerning Confucian thinking and learning expressed in poetry; whereas the latter represents texture of poetry, especially poetic structures, metrical schemes and rhythms, and other techniques of writing. Scholars of the Xingling School (School of Inner Self) of the Ming and Qing dynasties advocated rejecting dogmatic guidelines and expressing one's emotions and thoughts in literary works, while adherents of the Shenyun School (School of Elegant Subtlety) believed in subtlety and implicitness expressed through poetr y. Criticizing both literary trends, Weng promoted the principles and techniques of the Song-dynasty poetry. In terms of *yili,* he emphasized the need to follow classical Confucian tradition and erudition. In terms of *wenli,* he advocated exquisite intricacy, attention to details, and graceful structures with a great many variations, as well as the need to convey a substantive message. During the reign of Emperor Qianlong and Emperor Jiaqing of the Qing Dynasty, a boom in the study of Confucian classics and textual research led to the emergence of the Jili School (School of Reasoning and Structure). Weng advocated integration of form and content in poetry, thus promoting the development of poetry based on classic learning. However, his overemphasis on classic scholarliness in poetry was criticized by scholars of both his age and later generations.

CITATIONS

I don't care if my views differ from those of others, nor do I care if the differing views are from ancient scholars or my contemporaries. What I do care is analyzing carefully the structure and reasoning of writings in order to arrive at a balanced view. (Liu Xie: *The Literary Mind and the Carving of Dragons*)

Yili in Confucian classics is all about structure and reasoning in writing, i.e., the texture and proper presentation of writings. (Weng Fanggang: Preface to *Collection of My Works*)

Today's men of letters are in an era when Confucian studies are flourishing. It is therefore imperative that scholars base their study on research and verification, and that poets focus on the structure and reasoning of their works. (Weng Fanggang: Preface to *Collection of My Works*)

19

jiāngshān

江山

Rivers and Mountains / Country or State Power

The term, similar in meaning to *heshan* (河山), literarily means rivers and mountains. It is used to refer to the sovereignty of a state and all its territory. The term has these implications: rivers and mountains provide natural barriers that protect the country and its sovereignty; territory is the key feature of a state.

CITATION

To seize a region by force, establish a regime there, and extend its territory far and wide. (*The History of the Three Kingdoms*)

20

jiàohuà

教化

Shaping the Mind Through Education

Shaping the mind through education was a key concept of the political philosophy and an essential way of governance in ancient China. Rulers usually used a combination of means, both visible and invisible, to subtly spread their values among people so that these values would be observed in people's daily life, leading to integration of governance and social mores. These means include issuing administrative decrees, conducting moral education, creating a favorable environment, disseminating popular literature that promoted ethical values, and selecting officials through imperial examinations.

CITATION

Educating and influencing the people through *li* (礼) has the invisible impact of getting rid of immoral thoughts in the bud. (*The Book of Rites*)

21

jiǔzhōu
九州

Nine *Zhou* (Regions)

This term is an alternative designation for China. According to *The Book of History*, the country consisted of nine *zhou* (州), namely Jizhou, Yanzhou, Qingzhou, Xuzhou, Yangzhou, Jingzhou, Yuzhou, Liangzhou, and Yongzhou. There are similar references to the nine *zhou* in classic works of the same or later period, such as *The Rituals of Zhou*, *Er Ya*, and *Master Lü's Spring and Autumn Annals*. The nine *zhou* were never adopted as actual administrative divisions of the country, but they did show the general geographical area inhabited by the Chinese people since the late Spring and Autumn Period.

CITATIONS

The vitality of China depends on wind and thunder, unfortunately not a single horse's neighing is heard. I urge the Lord of Heaven to once again lift his spirits and, breaking all bonds and fetters, send talent of all kinds to the human world. (Gong Zizhen: *Miscellaneous Poems Written in the Year of 1839*)

As I see it, the cause of China's disasters lies not overseas but within the country. (Zhang Zhidong: Preface to Encouragement to Learning)

22

kējǔ

科举

The Imperial Civil Examination System

This is the system in which officials were selected through different levels of examinations. After Emperor Wen of the Sui Dynasty reunified China in 581, he abolished the system of selecting officials on the basis of family background or moral character. In 605, the first year of the reign of Emperor Yang of the Sui Dynasty, the system to select officials through imperial civil examinations was officially established. From then on, examination subjects, content, and recruitment standards varied from dynasty to dynasty. The *jinshi,* the highest level and the most difficult of imperial civil examinations, was always the most revered by scholars. In the Yuan and Ming dynasties, examination content was based on the Four Books and the Five Classics and had to be answered in the form of the "eight-legged" essay and refer to *Commentaries on the Four Books* and other classics. In 1905 Emperor Guangxu of the Qing Dynasty issued an edict abolishing the imperial civil examination system.

For 1,300 years since the Sui Dynasty, the imperial civil examination system was the main method for selecting officials, which had a broad and profound influence on Chinese society. It hastened the transformation of aristocracy-based politics to bureaucracy-based politics and had multiple functions such as educating people, selecting officials, choosing talent through examinations, social stratification, and carrying forward the traditional culture.

CITATIONS

Soon after Emperor Taizong of the Song Dynasty ascended the throne, he wanted to help people with both moral integrity and professional competence come to prominence, so he said to his ministers, "By recruiting remarkable people through the imperial civil examination system, I do not expect five out of ten of those recruited to excel. If one or two out of ten do, the imperial civil examination system can be used as an effective means to maintain political stability." (*The History of the Song Dynasty*)

The imperial civil examination system had to be implemented through schools, but those recommended by schools to official positions do not necessarily need to take the imperial civil examinations. (*The History of the Ming Dynasty*)

23

lài yǔ Xīshī, dào tōng wéi yī

厉与西施，道通为一

A Scabby Person and the Beautiful Lady Xishi Are the Same in the Eyes of Dao.

This is a famous statement made by Zhuangzi on how beauty is relative. Originally it meant there was no difference between a beauty and an ugly person, because they both came from and reflected Dao. The character 厉 (*lai*) meant 癞 (*lai*, covered in scabs) in ancient Chinese. Whether a person is beautiful or ugly is but a subjective perspective in the mind of the beholder. Besides, beauty can turn into ugliness, and vice versa. Zhuangzi, from the perspective of the origin of all things, stressed that beauty and ugliness are both in accord with Dao and are inherently the same. This idea has encouraged later literary critics to look at all things, including literary works, from the perspective that opposite things complement each other.

CITATIONS

In the light of Dao, a small blade of grass or a tall pillar, someone as ugly as a favus patient or someone as beautiful as Lady Xishi, as well as crafty and strange things, are all the same. (*Zhuangzi*)

Dao manifests in an array of objective things, but its genuine spirit lies within them. (Sikong Tu: Twenty-Four Styles of Poetry)

24

lè ér bù yín, āi ér bù shāng

乐而不淫，哀而不伤

Express Enjoyment Without Indulgence and Express Grief Without Excessive Distress

This is what Confucius said of the description of love between young men and women in the poem entitled "Guan Ju" in "Ballads of Zhounan," *The Book of Songs*. Later Confucian scholars regarded this as a basic requirement for poems and other literary works to advocate impartiality, peace of mind, and harmony between emotion and reason, making it a criterion for evaluating literary works. Its connotation is in accord with *zhongyong* (the golden mean) of Confucianism. In the more recent history, the connotation of the term has been continuously renewed to keep pace with the times.

CITATIONS

The poem "Guan Ju" expresses enjoyment without indulgence and grief without excessive distress. (*The Analects*)

Ballads from the states express passion of love without indulgence. Minor court hymns make complaints and criticisms without inciting trouble. (*Records of the Historian*)

25

lǐ

理

Li

The original meaning of *li* (理) was the texture of jade; later it was extended to contain three meanings: 1) the physical forms or proprieties of things, such as length, size, shape, tensile strength, weight, and color; 2) the universal laws followed by all things and beings; and 3) the original source or ontological existence of things. The last two meanings are similar to those of Dao. Scholars of the Song and Ming dynasties were particularly interested in describing and explaining the philosophy known as *li* (理), and considered it as the highest realm, giving rise to the School of Principle which dominated academic thought in the period from the Song to the Ming dynasties.

CITATIONS

Nothing happens at random; each follows its own *li* (laws). (Wang Bi: *A Brief Exposition of The Book of Changes*)

Everything exists according to its objective law but all things must follow the common *li* (law). (*Writings of the Cheng Brothers*)

26

lìyòng-hòushēng
利用厚生

Make Full Use of Resources to Enrich the People

The ancient Chinese believed that good governance allowed people to lead a life of plenty. The ruler should be frugal, not extravagant or wasteful. He should make good use of the country's material resources, reduce the corvée and tax burdens on the people so that they could live peaceful, prosperous, and happy lives. This belief was one of the sources of advocation for the people's livelihood and socialist thinking in modern China.

CITATION

A ruler should manifest his virtue in good governance, and the goal of governance is to bring a good life to the people... The ruler should act in an upright and virtuous manner, and ensure that the country's resources are put to good use and that the people live a prosperous life. These three goals complement one another. (*The Book of History*)

27

liángshǐ

良史

Trustworthy Historian / Factual History

This refers to historians or history books that record historical facts in an objective and truthful way based on evidences without covering up anything. Objectivity is the ultimate criterion for judging historians or history books in historiography.

CITATIONS

However, after reading a huge number of books, Liu Xiang and Yang Xiong came to view Sima Qian as a great historian... His accounts are straightforward and reasonable, accurate and substantive, and free from false praise; they do not cover up evil deeds. (*The Han History*)

A factual history is one which records both good and evil that have happened. (Su E: *Textual Studies by Su E*)

28

liángzhī
良知

Liangzhi (Conscience)

Humans are born with innate conscience and the ability to know and act upon it. The term *liangzhi* (良知) was first used by Mencius, who believed that what man knew by instinct was *liangzhi* (knowledge of goodness). The term includes *ren* (仁), i.e. love for one's parents and *yi* (义), i.e. respect for one's elder brothers. The concept is an important component of Mencius' belief in the innate goodness of human nature. The Ming-dynasty philosopher Wang Shouren raised the idea of "attaining *liangzhi*." He extended the Mencius' *liangzhi* to mean the principles of heaven, maintaining that all things under heaven and their laws were covered by *liangzhi*. With *liangzhi* being extended to its fullest (through self-cultivation and moral practice), it is possible to know and put in practice all moral truths.

CITATIONS

What is known without thinking is the innate knowledge of goodness. (*Mencius*)

Principles of heaven and conscience are the same in essence. (*Records of Great Learning*)

29

liù jīng jiē shǐ

六经皆史

The Six Confucian Classics Are All About History.

The Six Confucian Classics are *The Book of Changes*, *The Book of History*, *The Book of Songs*, *The Book of Rites*, *The Book of Music*, and *The Spring and Autumn Annals*. An important proposition put forward by scholars of late imperial China was that those are all historical texts. According to these scholars, the Six Classics are all concerned with the social and political realities of the Xia, Shang, and Zhou dynasties rather than the teachings left by ancient sages. Zhang Xuecheng of the Qing Dynasty was the representative scholar to systematically expound this proposition. This view challenged the sacred status of the classics of Confucianism and marked a self-conscious and independent trend in Chinese historiography.

CITATION

Scholars worship the Six Classics and say that they are the words of sages set down to teach later generations. They do not realize that the classics are the regulations and historical facts recorded by officials in the flourishing days of the three dynasties of Xia, Shang, and Zhou. They are not the writings of ancient sages. (Zhang Xuecheng: *General Principles of Literature and History*)

30

liùyì

六义

The Six Basic Elements

The six basic elements were drawn from *The Book of Songs* by scholars of the Han Dynasty to promote the state's governance, social enlightenment, and education. The six are: *feng* (ballad), which offers an insight into the influence of a sage's thinking on ordinary folk customs; *fu* (narrative), which directly states the goodness or evilness of court politics; *bi* (analogy), which criticizes mildly the inadequacies of court politics by comparing one thing with another; *xing* (association), which extols a virtue by making an indirect reference to some other laudable thing; *ya* (court hymn), which shows the proper way of acquitting oneself as a norm for posterity to follow; and *song* (eulogy), which praises and promotes vir tue. All the six elements were originally used by Confucian scholars to expound on the creative techniques in *The Book of Songs*. Later, they were used to emphasize creative styles of all works of poetry. They also served as essential principles of literary criticism.

CITATION

A ballad tells how to run the country via the customs and folkways that have survived through the ages. A narrative flatly states the positive and negative things in state affairs. An analogy is made when one sees a vice in court politics but dares not directly point it out; it hints at the vice by describing something similar to it. An association, in view of the clean and honest governance of the time, voices its appreciation and support through borrowing from some other commendable thing, in order to avoid arousing suspicions of unscrupulous flattery. A court hymn is related to propriety, describing something rightly done and setting norms for people of later generations to observe. A eulogy praises and promotes a reigning monarch's virtues by admiring his elegant, upright manner. (Zheng Xuan: *Annotations on The Rites of Zhou*)

31

měicì
美刺

Extolment and Satirical Criticism

This literary term is used in poetry to comment on a ruler's moral character, policies, decrees, and performance, either in praise or criticism. Confucius was the first to point out that poetry could be used to vent resentment and thus established a basic function of poetry writing by emphasizing the role *The Book of Songs* played in voicing grievances. In the Han Dynasty, however, poetry tended to be used as a vehicle for extolling the accomplishments and virtues of rulers. In "Preface to *Mao's Version of The Book of Songs*" and "Preface to *On the Categories of The Book of Songs*," two influential writings on theory of poetry published during the Han Dynasty, extolment and satirical criticism was regarded as an underlying principle of poetic criticism. This principle was widely employed by poets and writers of later generations as a way of getting involved in politics and making their impact on the society. This constituted a fundamental function and an essential feature of Chinese literature.

CITATIONS

Poems are composed to applaud the rulers to continue to do what is good by extolling their achievements and virtues, and to urge them to change the erroneous course by satirizing and criticizing their wrong doings. (Zheng Xuan: Preface to *On the Categories of The Book of Songs*)

To Confucian scholars in the Han Dynasty, poetry has two basic functions: extolment and satirical criticism. (Cheng Tingzuo: *Qingxi Collection*)

32

mín wéi bāng běn
民惟邦本

People Being the Foundation of the State

This term means that the people are the essence of the state or the foundation upon which it stands. Only when people live and work in peace and contentment can the state be peaceful and stable. This saying, which first appeared in a pseudo-version of *The Classical Book of History* as an instruction by Yu the Great, can be traced to Mencius' statement: "The essence of a state is the people, next come the god of land and the god of grain (which stand for state power), and the last the ruler," and Xunzi's statement, "Just as water can float a boat, so can water overturn it." This idea gave rise to the "people first" thought advocated by Confucianism.

CITATION

Our ancestor Yu the Great warned: (a ruler) must maintain a close relationship with the people; he must not regard them as insignificant. They are the foundation of a state, and a state can enjoy peace only when its foundation is firm. (*The Book of History*)

33

qì

气

Qi (Vital Force)

Qi (vital force) has a material existence independent of subjective consciousness and is the basic element of all physical beings. It is also the basis for the birth and existence of life and spirit. In addition, some thinkers have given a moral attribute to *qi*. *Qi* is in constant motion and change, and has no specific shape. Its concentration gives birth to a thing and its evaporation signals the end of that thing. *Qi* permeates all physical beings and their surroundings. *Qi*, as a philosophical concept, is different from what is commonly understood by the word *qi* (气), namely, air. Although things in liquid or solid form are different from things in air form, from the perspective of the ancient Chinese philosophy, their formation and existence are the results of the concentration of *qi*.

CITATIONS

It is *qi* that permeates everything under heaven. (*Zhuangzi*)

The convergence of *qi* of heaven and that of earth gives life to all things. (Wang Chong: *A Comparative Study of Different Schools of Learning*)

34

qíng
情

Qing

The term has three different meanings. First, it means human emotions and desires, referring to the natural and instinctive reaction to external circumstances, not a learned response. Second, it refers to specific human emotions and desires, commonly known as the six human emotions: love, hatred, happiness, anger, sadness, and joy, or as the seven human emotions: happiness, anger, sadness, fear, love, hatred, and desire. Third, it means the true state of affairs, or actual situation. For centuries, scholars have had different interpretations on the first two meanings. Some advocated that emotions should be restrained or controlled, while others believed that emotions and desires were natural and should be properly guided.

CITATIONS

What are human emotions? They are happiness, anger, sadness, fear, love, hatred, and desire that arise instinctively. (*The Book of Rites*)

If those in high positions act in good faith, the people will not dare to conceal the truths. (*The Analects*)

35

qíngjǐng
情景

Sentiment and Scenery

This term refers to the mutual dependence and integration of an author's description of scenery and objects, and his expression of feelings in his literary creation. *Qing* (情) is an author's inner feelings, and *jing* (景) refers to external scenery or an object. The theory of sentiment and scenery stresses integration of the two, maintaining that sentiment can hardly be aroused without scenery and that scenery or an object cannot be appreciated without sentiment. This term appeared in the Song Dynasty. Compared with earlier notions about sentiment and scenery, this one is more emphatic about fusing the depiction of scenery with the expression of feelings, and the process of creation with that of appreciation.

CITATIONS

Scenery has no place in poetry unless there are feelings for it; feelings cannot be stirred without the inspiration of scenery. (Fan Xiwen: *Midnight Dialogues Across Two Beds*)

Sentiment and scenery seem to be two distinct things, but in fact they cannot be separated. A good poet k nows how to integrate them seamlessly. An ingenious combination of sentiment and scenery means scenery embedded in sentiment and vice versa. (Wang Fuzhi: *Desultory Remarks on Poetry from Ginger Studio*)

36

qù
趣

Qu

Qu is the aspirations, emotions, and interests expressed in the work of a writer or artist. His pursuit of *qu* determines his unique perception and comprehension of nature and life. It also determines what theme he chooses for his work and how he gives expression to it. *Qu* is invisible but manifests its value and appeal through aesthetic appreciation.

CITATIONS

Ji Kang was good at explaining profundities and writing. He had a high style and fine taste. A forthright and broad-minded man, indeed! (*The Jin History*)

The only thing really hard to understand in the world is *qu*. *Qu* is like the hues of hills, the taste of water, the splendor of flowers, or the beauty of a woman. Even an eloquent person can hardly find words to put it clearly. Only those with empathy know it well… *Qu* that comes from nature is deep and mellow; if it comes from book learning, it is often shallow. (Yuan Hongdao: Preface to Chen Zhengfu's *Inspirations of the Mind*)

37

rénwén-huàchéng

人文化成

Ren Wen Hua Cheng

The term is used to describe efforts to teach people essential ideals and principles of *ren wen* (人文) and guide them to embrace goodness with the aim of building a harmonious – albeit hierarchical – social order, according to the level of development of a civilization and the specifics of the society. *Ren wen* refers to poetry, books, social norms, music, law, and other non-material components of civilization. *Hua* (化) means to edify the populace; *cheng* (成) refers to the establishment or prosperity of rule by civil means (as opposed to force). The concept emphasizes rule by civil means, and is another expression of the Chinese concept of "civilization."

CITATION

Observing the movements of the sun, moon, and stars helps us learn about the change of seasons; studying the development of poetry, books, social norms, and music enables us to edify the populace so that the rule by civil means can prosper. (*The Book of Changes*)

38

rénzhì

人治

Rule by Man

Rule by man, as opposed to rule by law, is the most important ruling concept in the Confucian political philosophy in ancient China. It calls for ruling a state and its people through orderly human relations, moral standards, and other value systems. Rule by man emphasizes the fundamental role and importance of people in conducting political affairs. It emphasizes that a ruler should have a lofty and noble character, select competent officials with integrity to run the state, and educate and influence the general public. In Chinese history, this concept of governance was designed to achieve a harmonious relationship between the sovereign, his officials, and his subjects, which meant "benevolent governance."

CITATIONS

Rule by man aims to regulate human relations. (Zheng Xuan: *Annotations on The Book of Rites*)

Rule by man, in the final analysis, is to regulate human emotions and desires; it is the reason and basis for developing social norms and music education. (Wang Chong: *A Comparative Study of Different Schools of Learning*)

39

rén

仁

Ren

The basic meaning of the term is love for others. Its extended meaning refers to the state of harmony among people, and the unity of all things under heaven. *Ren* (仁) constitutes the foundation and basis for moral behavior. It is also a consciousness that corresponds to the norms of moral behavior. Roughly put, *ren* has the following three implications: 1) compassion or conscience; 2) virtue of respect built upon the relationship between fathers and sons and among brothers; and 3) the unity of all things under heaven. Confucianism holds *ren* as the highest moral principle. *Ren* is taken as love in the order of first showing filial piety to one's parents and elder brothers, and then extending love and care to other members of the family, and eventually to everyone else under heaven.

CITATIONS

Ren means to restrain one's self and follow social norms. (*The Analects*)

Ren is the principle of love and the moral nature of human mind. (Zhu Xi: *The Analects Variorum*)

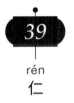

40

rìxīn
日新

Constant Renewal

This term refers to an ongoing process of self-renewal, which also brings new life to the people, society, and the nation. This process features continuous progress and improvement. It represents a tenacious and innovative spirit that permeates all levels of "self-cultivation, family regulation, state governance, bringing peace to all under heaven."

CITATION

"If we can improve ourselves in one day, we should do so every day, and keep building on improvement," reads the inscription on the bathtub of Tang, founder of the Shang Dynasty. "People should be encouraged to discard the old and embrace the new, give up evil ideas, and live up to high moral standards," says *The Book of History*. "Though it was an ancient state, Zhou saw its future lying in continuously renewing itself," comments *The Book of Songs*. Therefore, *junzi* (men of virtue) should strive to excel themselves in all aspects and at all times. (*The Book of Rites*)

41

róngcái

镕裁

Refining and Deleting

This term refers to improving a literary work by refining its basic content and making the presentation concise. Refining and deleting is a basic process in literary writing. The term was first mentioned in *The Literary Mind and the Carving of Dragons*. It means that in producing a literary work, the author should select the right elements from all the material he has, delete unnecessary parts and keep the essence, and write in a concise way to best present what he has in mind and to best suit the styles of writing. It shows that literary creation is a process of constantly striving for perfection in terms of both content and form. This idea had a great impact on the theory of theatrical writing in the Ming and Qing dynasties.

CITATIONS

Refining means to shape the basic content and structure of a literary work, while deleting means to cut off redundant words or sentences. Once done, the essay will be well structured, with a clear-cut theme. (Liu Xie: *The Literary Mind and the Carving of Dragons*)

Xie Ai's essays are ornate in expression yet free of unnecessary sentences or words, with nothing to be deleted. Wang Ji's writing is concise in style; it sufficiently expresses an idea without the need for using more words. Men of letters like them surely command the art of refining and deleting by using a proper amount of words and expressions. (Liu Xie: *The Literary Mind and the Carving of Dragons*)

42

shèjì

社稷

Sheji (Gods of the Earth and the Five Grains)

She (社) is the God of the Earth, and *ji* (稷 millet), represents the God of the Five Grains. Chinese kings and vassals of ancient times offered sacrifices to these gods. As the Han Chinese depended on farming, these gods were the most important primitive objects of worship. The ancient rulers offered sacrifices to the gods of the Earth and the Five Grains every year to pray for peace and good harvests in the country. As a result, *sheji* became a symbol of the nation and state power.

CITATION

Why do the Sons of Heaven worship the gods of the Earth and the Five Grains? They do so to seek blessings for all under heaven and to requite the gods' blessings. Without earth, people have nowhere to live; without grain, people have nothing to eat. The earth is too vast to be worshipped everywhere; the variety of grains is too large to be worshipped one by one. Therefore, earth altars to the God of the Earth have been set up to honor the earth; and as millet is the chief one of the five grains, it has become the God of the Five Grains and sacrifices have been instituted. (*Debates of the White Tiger Hall*)

43

shén
神

Shen (Spirit / Spiritual)

The term has four meanings. First, it indicates a deity in a personified sense, possessing superhuman capabilities. Natural things, such as heaven and earth, mountains and rivers, sun and moon, and stars, have their deity. A human soul may also become a deity after death. Second, it indicates the human spirit and mind. Daoism considers "spirit" to be the dominating factor in human life. Therefore, maintaining and refining the spirit is most important to prolong life. Third, it indicates the subtle and unfathomable changing of all things as well as heaven and earth occurring under the interaction of yin and yang. In this sense the term is often used together with *hua* (化 change), the combination being called "divine change." Fourth, it indicates a marvelous and unfathomable realm in life attained by a person.

CITATIONS

The nation will prosper when people's opinions are heard and it will perish when only the will of the spirit is followed. (*Zuo's Commentary on The Spring and Autumn Annals*)

In *qi* (vital force) there are yin and yang whose gradual operation means change. The unpredictable interaction and unity of yin and yang is what is called spirit. (Zhang Zai: *Enlightenment Through Confucian Teachings*)

Being sage beyond understanding, that is called divine. (*Mencius*)

44

shénsī

神思

Imaginative Contemplation

The term refers to a state of mind in the process of literary and artistic creation. It suggests that the author, fully inspired by emotions, transcends the constraint of time and space, and enters into a state of free imagination or a special mood for literary and artistic creation, before producing a natural and beautiful work of literature or art, either in language or in imagery. This term was popularly used in literary and artistic theories of the Wei, Jin, and Southern and Northern dynasties. Liu Xie of the Southern Dynasties devoted one chapter especially to this term in *The Literary Mind and the Carving of Dragons*. With emphasis on the unique mental activity in literar y and ar tistic creation, imaginative contemplation is different from other cognitive activities.

CITATIONS

An ancient saying goes, "Though he lives among the common folks, deep in his heart he concerns himself with affairs of the imperial court." This is called imaginative contemplation. When one writes, his imaginations and thoughts may transcend time and space. (Liu Xie: *The Literary Mind and the Carving of Dragons*)

The guiding principles for literary creation come from imaginative contemplation. Man's feelings and thoughts about the external world are formless and highly changeable. (Xiao Zixian: *The History of Southern Qi*)

45

shēng yī wú tīng, wù yī wú wén
声一无听，物一无文

A Single Note Does Not Compose a Melodious Tune, Nor Does a Single Color Make a Beautiful Pattern.

This statement suggests that the beauty of literature and art lies in the unity and harmony of diverse elements. It became an important principle in ancient Chinese theories on literature and art, and facilitated the development of literature and art.

CITATIONS

A single note does not compose a melodious tune; a single color does not form a beautiful pattern; a single flavor does not make a delicious meal; and a single thing has nothing to compare with. (*Discourses on Governance of the States*)

It is natural that silk of different colors can be used to embroider a beautiful pattern, different notes to produce melodious music, and expressions of different feelings to present a fine work of literary art. (Liu Xie: *The Literary Mind and the Carving of Dragons*)

46

shèng

圣

Sage / Sageness

The term refers to the highest realm of human integrity and morality, hence one who has reached this state is a sage. It is often used in relation to "wisdom," since one who is a wise man understands the way of man, while one who is a sage understands the way of heaven. Thus a sage with knowledge of the way of heaven will interact successfully with other people.

CITATIONS

He who listens to the principles of men of virtue is wise; he who not only listens but also understands them is a sage. The sage understands the way of heaven. (*Wuxing*, from the bamboo slips unearthed from a Chu State tomb at Guodian)

Confucius was a sage who was able to seize the opportunity of his era. (*Mencius*)

47

shī yán zhì
诗言志

Poetry Expresses Aspirations.

A poem expresses aspirations in one's heart. *Zhi* (志) here means the author's aspirations, emotions, and thoughts. The concept of "poetry expressing aspirations," first seen in the Confucian classic *The Book of History*, was hailed by Zhu Ziqing as the "manifesto" of Chinese poetry. Enriched by poetry critics through the generations, it was later established as a basic concept in Chinese literary criticism.

CITATIONS

Poems express aspirations deep in one's heart, whereas songs are verses for chanting. (*The Book of History*)

Poems come from aspirations. An aspiration in hear t is an aspiration; an aspiration in words is a poem. (Preface to *The Book of Songs*)

48

shī yuán qíng

诗缘情

Poetry Springs from Emotions.

Poems originate from the poet's heart-felt feelings. Lu Ji of the Western Jin Dynasty said in "The Art of Writing" that a poet must have a surge of feeling deep in his heart before he could create a poem. This view, complementing the concept of "poetry expressing aspirations," stresses the lyrical and aesthetic nature of literary works and echoes the evolution of literary tastes during the Wei and Jin dynasties. "Poetry springing from emotions" represents another viewpoint on the nature of poetry and literature in ancient China.

CITATIONS

Poetry, springing from emotions, reads beautifully in its form of expression. (Lu Ji: The Art of Writing)

Everyone has diverse feelings, and he expresses his feelings and aspirations in a poetical way when he is stimulated by the external world and his heart is touched. All poems come from natural emotions. (Liu Xie: *The Literary Mind and the Carving of Dragons*)

49

shǐ cái sān cháng

史才三长

Three Strengths of a Good Historian

According to the renowned historiographer Liu Zhiji of the Tang Dynasty, those who study and write history must have three strengths, namely, the ability to compose historical works, rich knowledge of history and historical materials, and deep insight that enables them to analyze and evaluate history. Liu believed that deep insight in analyzing and commenting on history was the most important of the three qualifications.

CITATION

A historian must have three strengths. ...The three strengths are talent, learning, and insight. (*The Old Tang History*)

50

shūyuàn
书院

Classical Academy

Classical academies were cultural and educational institutions that existed in China from the Tang and Song dynasties through the Ming and Qing dynasties. They were established either by the public or the government to serve the multiple purposes of education, research, and library service. Their origins were Buddhist monasteries and private libraries in the Tang Dynasty. Classical academies flourished in the Song Dynasty. In the early years of the Southern Song Dynasty, Zhu Xi, Zhang Shi, Lü Zuqian, Lu Jiuyuan, and some other scholars established academies that served as teaching and research centers of their respective schools of thought. The academies were independent of government schools and were located mostly in tranquil and scenic places. Under the supervision of learned Confucian scholars, the academies pursued academic freedom and innovation. Teachers taught by both precept and example, and laid stress on shaping their students' moral character, rather than encouraging them to win degrees in the imperial civil examination system. By the end of the Southern Song Dynasty, however, the academies became increasingly government-oriented and were linked with the imperial civil examination system. The rise and decline of the academies was in harmony with the rise and decline of the School of Principle during the Song and Ming dynasties.

In 1901 the Qing government ordered all the academies be changed to schools in modern sense. Having existed for more than 1,000 years, the academies greatly helped develop traditional Chinese culture and education, and convey Chinese culture abroad.

CITATION

Places where earlier Confucian scholars taught, or where distinguished men of virtue lived and left behind stories and legacies, or wealthy families who were willing to support scholars with money and food, could all contribute to the establishment of classical academies. (*The History of the Yuan Dynasty*)

51

shùntiān-yìngrén

顺天应人

Follow the Mandate of Heaven and Comply with the Wishes of the People

The ancient Chinese believed that virtuous men followed the will of heaven in establishing a political regime and becoming its sovereigns; hence their success came from the mandate of heaven. This thought is similar to the Western notion of the divine right of kings; but it also emphasizes the wishes and will of the people, or people-centered thinking. In ancient China, this phrase was often used in praise of the founding of a new dynasty, and the implementation of major social reforms to justify its legitimacy.

CITATION

Changes of yin and yang in heaven and earth give rise to the four seasons. Following the mandate of heaven and complying with the wishes of the people, King Tang and King Wu overthrew old regimes and established the Shang and Zhou dynasties respectively. (*The Book of Changes*)

52

tàijí
太极

Taiji (The Supreme Ultimate)

Taiji (the supreme ultimate) has three different meanings. First, it refers to the origin of the world. The ancient Chinese saw it either as *qi* (vital force) or *yuanqi* (primordial vital force) that permeates the chaotic world, or as a universal principle, i.e. Dao or *li* (理), or as *wu* (无). Second, it is used as a term of divination, referring to the initial state before divinatory numbers, the odd number one (written as —) and the even number two (written as – –), are applied or before the yarrow stems are divided. Divination is conducted on the basis of *taiji*. Third, it stands for the highest point or boundary of space.

CITATIONS

Changes evolve from *taiji,* which gives rise to two primal forces of yin and yang. They in turn give birth to heaven and earth. (*An Alternative Explanation of The Book of Changes*)

Taiji is the overriding law of all things, as well as heaven and earth. (*Classified Conversations of Master Zhu Xi*)

53

tàixué
太学

Imperial Academy

The imperial academy was the highest educational institution and educational administrative department in feudal China. The term first appeared in the Western Zhou Dynasty, but the first imperial academy was not officially established until 124 BC during the reign of Emperor Wu of the Han Dynasty. Teachers of the imperial academy were called "grand academicians" (literarily "scholars of broad learning"). They were well versed in Confucian classics, had rich teaching experience, and possessed both moral integrity and professional competence. Their students were called "students of the imperial academy" or "students of the grand academicians." At its peak the imperial academy had 10,000 students.

The central governments of all subsequent dynasties, including the Ming and Qing, had an imperial academy or a similar institution of education, usually located in the capital. It had different names and systems in different dynasties. The imperial academy, the top institution of learning run by the central government, along with local institutions of education and private schools, formed a complete education system in ancient China. They were significant in disseminating the Confucian classics and ancient China's mainstream values with Confucianism as its main school of thought.

CITATION

May I propose Your Majesty establish an imperial academy where teachers well versed in the Confucian classics can train students from all over the country. (*The History of the Han Dynasty*)

54

tǐxìng
体性

Style and Temperament

This is an important term about literary style that stresses the unity and integration of the styles of writings with the temperaments of their authors. The term originated from Liu Xie's *The Literary Mind and the Carving of Dragons*. One chapter of the book discusses how the styles of writings are related to the temperaments of the writers, and argues that the writings truly reflect the temperaments of their authors. This has encouraged later generations to analyze different styles of literary works based on the authors' temperaments and became a basic line of thought on ancient Chinese literary style.

CITATIONS

When emotions stir, they take the form of language. When ideas emerge, they are expressed in writings. Thus the obscure becomes manifest and the internal feelings pour into the open. However, talent may be mediocre or outstanding, temperament masculine or feminine, learning deep or shallow, upbringing refined or vulgar. All this results from differences in nature and nurture. Hence the unusual cloud-like variations in the realm of writing and the mysterious wave-like undulations in the garden of literature. (Liu Xie: *The Literary Mind and the Carving of Dragons*)

So it is natural that those with an open and easy-going temperament create poems with tonal rhythms that are direct, smooth, and easy to understand; those with a slow temperament write in relaxed tonal rhythms; those with a broad mind, magnificent and uninhibited; those with a heroic character, powerful and gallant; those with a depressed personality, sad and miserable; those with a weird temperament, out of the ordinary. Temperament decides the tonal rhythms of an author's writings. People have their own emotions and personalities. How can all the poems be judged by the same standard for tonal rhythms? (Li Zhi: My Understanding of Poetic Genre)

55

tǐyòng

体用

Ti and *Yong*

Ti (体) and *yong* (用) can be understood in three different ways: 1) a physical thing and its functions or roles; 2) the ontological existence of a thing and its expression and application; and 3) the fundamental code of conduct, and its observance. In any *ti–yong* relationship, *ti* provides the basis on which *yong* depends.

CITATIONS

Tian (天) means heaven in the physical sense, while *qian* (乾) means its functions and significance. (Kong Yingda: *Correct Meaning of The Book of Changes*)

What is most subtle is *li* (理), while what is most conspicuous is *xiang* (象). *Li* as the ontological existence and *xiang* as its manifestation are of the same origin; there is no difference between them. (Cheng Yi: *Cheng Yi's Commentary on The Book of Changes*)

56

tiān

天

Tian (Heaven)

Tian (天) is a sacred and fundamental concept in ancient Chinese philosophy. It has three different meanings. The first is the physical sky or the entirety of nature (not including human society), the operations of which manifest certain laws and order. The second refers to a spiritual being, which possesses an anthropomorphic will and governs everything in the universe. The third denotes the universal law, which is observed by all things and beings, and which is also the basis of human nature, morality, and social and political orders.

CITATIONS

Nature's ways are constant. They did not exist because Yao was on the throne or disappear because Jie was the ruler. (*Xunzi*)

Heaven trusts and blesses the people. (*The Book of History*)

Heaven is the overarching law of the universe. (*Writings of the Cheng Brothers*)

57

tiānxià

天下

Tianxia (All Under Heaven)

This term referred mainly to all the land under the name of the Son of Heaven and the right to rule on such land. The ancient Chinese held that the rule of senior officials was over their enfeoffed land, and that of dukes and princes was over feudal states. The rule of the Son of Heaven was over all the land. Literally, *tianxia* (天下) means "all under heaven." It actually refers to all the territory embracing the enfeoffed land and feudal states under the rule or in the name of the Son of Heaven, as well as all the subjects and the right to rule. The term has later evolved to refer to the whole natin or the whole world.

CITATIONS

All land under heaven falls within the domain of the Son of Heaven; all those on this land are his subjects. (*The Book of Songs*)

With little popular support, even his relatives will betray and desert him; but with massive popular support, everyone under heaven will pledge allegiance to him. (*Mencius*)

The rise and fall of a nation is the concern of every citizen. (Liang Qichao: *Collections of Ice Drinking Study*)

58

wáng

王

King

King was originally the title for the "Son of Heaven," namely, the country's supreme ruler in the Xia, Shang and Zhou dynasties. From the Spring and Autumn Period onward, the power of the Zhou court gradually weakened and the kingdom disintegrated. By the time of the Warring States Period, any monarch could call himself a king. Up to the Qin and Han dynasties, king became the highest title granted by the emperor to a male member of the imperial family. In the political philosophical discourse of Confucianism, especially in the works of Confucius and Mencius, a king represents heaven's will and therefore ought to have supreme, unchallengeable power; at the same time, he is imbued with a high moral attribute and political ideals. According to Confucianism, to be a king is to unify or govern the country with benevolence and righteousness, or to win over people by morally justified means. Likewise, the pursuit of the kingly way means using benevolent and righteous means to unify and govern the country.

CITATION

He to whom the people swear allegiance can rule as a king; he perishes when the people desert him. (*Xunzi*)

59

wángdào

王道

Kingly Way (Benevolent Governance)

Confucianism advocates the political principle of governing the country through benevolence and winning people's support through virtue as opposed to *badao* (霸道) – the despotic way. Enlightened kings and emperors of ancient times governed the country primarily through benevolence and virtue. In the Warring States Period, Mencius advocated this idea as a political concept: Only by governing the state with benevolence and righteousness, and by handling state-to-state relations on the basis of virtue, can a ruler win popular support and subsequently unify the country. The kingly way or benevolent governance epitomizes the Chinese people's respect for "civilization" and their opposition to the use of force and tyranny.

CITATIONS

By upholding justice without any partiality or bias, the kingly way is inclusive and boundless. (*The Book of History*)

One who governs by force through feigning virtue may gain only hegemonic dominance, and hegemony must have a large state as its basis; one who governs through virtue and benevolence is a king who does not necessarily need a large state... Allegiance commanded through force from the people does not mean the conquest of their heart; it is only because they are not strong enough to revolt. Allegiance gained through benevolence and virtue is really from the heart of the people, who will follow whole-heartedly, just like that of the seventy-two disciples of Confucius. (*Mencius*)

60

wéi zhèng yǐ dé

为政以德

Governance Based on Virtue

Governance of a state should be guided by virtue. Confucius expounded this philosophy – which his followers in later eras promoted – on the basis of the approach advocated by the rulers in the Western Zhou Dynasty that prized high moral values and the virtue of being cautious in meting out punishment. Governance based on virtue stands in contrast to rule by use of harsh punishment as a deterrent. It does not, however, exclude the use of punishment, but rather highlights the decisive role of virtue in governance, and regards moral edification both as the fundamental principle and the essential means for achieving good governance.

CITATION

Governance based on virtue is like the North Star taking its place in the sky, while all the other stars revolve around it. (*The Analects*)

61

wénmíng

文明

Wenming (Civilization)

This term refers to a thriving, prosperous, and perceptibly refined society in which people behave in a cultured fashion. *Wen* (文) refers to the arts and humanities, including social norms, music education, moral cultivation, and a social order that is hierarchical yet harmonious. *Ming* (明) means bright, prosperous, and highly civilized. The Chinese nation has always preferred *wen* to *wu* (武 force). This is the loftiest ideal pursued by the Chinese nation since ancient times. It was also the criterion by which to judge whether the governance of a nation was well conducted.

CITATION

In a civilized society weapons are destroyed and war ceases. (Jiao Gong: *Annotations on The Book of Changes*)

62

wénqì

文气

Wenqi

Wenqi (文气) is the personality an author demonstrates in his works, and is a fusion of his innate temperament and the vitality seen in his works. Originally, *qi* (气) referred to the basic element in the initial birth and formation of all things, as well as heaven and earth. In literary criticism, it refers to an author's distinctive individuality and its manifestation in his writings. Humans are believed to develop different characters and traits endowed by the *qi* of heaven and earth. Reflected in literary creation, such different characters and traits naturally find expression in distinctive styles and varying degrees of vigor as well as rhythm and cadence.

CITATIONS

Literary writing is governed by *qi*. Either clear or murky, *qi* determines the temperament of a writer, refined or vulgar, and his talent, high or low. *Qi* cannot be acquired. (Cao Pi: *On Literary Classics*)

If a writer has a strong inner flow of *qi*, the length of his sentences will be well-balanced, and his choice of tone and cadence will just be right. (Han Yu: A Letter of Response to Li Yi)

63

wén yǐ zài dào
文以载道

Literature Is the Vehicle of Ideas.

This term is a Confucian statement about the relationship between literature and ideas. *Wen* (文) refers to literary creations and works, while *dao* (道) refers to the ideas conveyed by literary works. Writers and philosophers in ancient China explicated these ideas as Confucian thought and ethics. Han Yu (leader of the mid- Tang-dynasty movement advocating the prose style of the Qin and Han dynasties) and some others proposed that the purpose of writings should be in line with the classics of the ancient sages as well as promote them. Zhou Dunyi, a neo-Confucian philosopher of the Song Dynasty, expounded the principle of literature serving as a vehicle of ideas. He concluded that literature was like a vehicle while ideas were like goods loaded on it, and that literature was nothing but a means and a vehicle to convey Confucian ideas. This theory was valuable because it stressed the social role of literature and emphasized that writers should know what they were writing about to ensure that their works conveyed correct ideas. However, it underestimated the aesthetic value of literature and later met opposition from thinkers and writers who emphasized the value of literature per se.

CITATION

Writings are meant to convey ideas and ethics. When vehicles are not used, even if the wheels and shafts are excessively decorated, it is simply a waste. Fine language is only a means for writing, whereas ethics are the essence of writings. (Zhou Dunyi: *The Gist of Confucian Thought*)

64

wúwéi

无为

Non-action

Wuwei (non-action) refers to a state of action. Daoism contrasts "action" to "non-action." "Action" generally means that the rulers impose their will on others or the world without showing any respect for or following the intrinsic nature of things. "Non-action" is the opposite of "action," and has three main points: 1) through self-control containing the desire to interfere; 2) following the nature of all things and the people; and 3) bringing into play the initiative of all things and people. "Non-action" does not mean not doing anything, but is a wiser way of doing things. Non-action leads to the result of getting everything done.

CITATIONS

Sages deal with things through non-action and teach ordinary people through non-speech. (*Laozi*)

Dao always makes all things possible through non-interference with them. (*Laozi*)

65

wǔxíng

五行

Wuxing

There are three meanings to the term. 1) The five fundamental things or elements that make up all things. *The Book of History* was the first to define the five elements: metal, wood, water, fire, and earth. Each of these has its own properties and they interact in a generative or destructive relationship. 2) On a more abstract level, the term refers to the basic framework to understand the world. All things can be included in the realm of *wuxing* (五行) and their properties are explained or understood accordingly. 3) It refers to five kinds of moral behavior. Xunzi once criticized Zisi and Mencius for "creating *wuxing* on the basis of old theories." Ancient bamboo slips unearthed from a grave at Guodian dating back to the State of Chu as well as inscribed silk texts from the Mawangdui Tomb of the Western Han Dynasty, all describe this *wuxing* as benevolence, righteousness, *li* (礼), wisdom, and the wisdom and character of a sage.

CITATIONS

In heaven there are the sun, moon, and stars, while on earth there are the five elements: metal, wood, water, fire, and earth. (*Zuo's Commentary on The Spring and Autumn Annals*)

The *qi* of heaven and that of earth merge into one; it evolves into yin and yang, the four seasons, and the five elements of metal, wood, water, fire, and earth. (Dong Zhongshu: *Luxuriant Gems of The Spring and Autumn Annals*)

66

wù

物

Wu (Thing / Matter)

Wu (物) usually denotes an existence in the universe that has a form or an image. In general, the word has three different meanings. First, it refers to any concrete existence, encompassing all natural and man-made objects, all organisms and human beings. Second, it covers interpersonal matters and activities such as taking care of one's parents, entering politics, or managing state affairs. In this sense, *wu* means "matter." Third, the word sums up all existing physical and social matters, generally called "everything."

CITATIONS

First, there is the universe. Then everything comes into being and fills up the universe. (*The Book of Changes*)

Conscience must relate to "things," which refer to various matters. If one's conscience is applied to parents, then taking care of one's parents is the "matter." (*Records of Great Learning*)

67

xiàng wài zhī xiàng, jǐng wài zhī jǐng
象外之象，景外之景

The Image Beyond an Image, the Scene Beyond a Scene

Readers of poetry create images and scenes in their minds based on what they are reading. These are the readers' imaginations based on what is depicted in the poems. The term comes from Daoist theories about the relationships between discourses, ideas or meanings, and images that symbolize profound meaning in *The Book of Changes*. From the Wei, Jin to the Tang Dynasty, poetry critics sought "the image beyond an image, the scene beyond a scene" in order to pursue the spiritual implications and the beauty of images that are beyond textual descriptions. This term gives expression to the artistic and aesthetic tastes and ideals of the Chinese nation.

CITATIONS

The imagery of poets is like the sunshine warming Lantian so that fine jades under its ground issue smoke: They can be seen from afar but not observed right before your eyes. The image beyond an image, the scene beyond a scene – are they not simply beyond words! (Sikong Tu: Letter to Wang Jipu)

That which makes a poem a poem is a poetic appeal beyond the image, an image beyond the words and words saying things beyond their meaning. (Peng Lu: Preface to *Collected Poems of Peng Lu*)

68

xiéhé-wànbāng

协和万邦

Coexistence of All in Harmony

The term refers to the exercise of benevolent government by virtuous and wise rulers in ancient China to win the allegiance of all the vassals, so as to achieve an integration and acculturation of different ethnic groups and create a harmonious and unified alliance of tribes or a multi-ethnic state. Harmonious coexistence of all is a key feature of the concept of social harmony in Chinese culture and one of the core values of the Chinese nation.

CITATION

(Emperor Yao) was able to promote moral values, so that amity prevailed in his clan. He then clarified the hierarchical order of tribal officials. Only when this was done could all vassal states, big and small, prosper in harmony, and the people become friendly with each other. (*The Book of History*)

69

xīn

心

Heart / Mind

The heart, a vital organ of life, underpins one's emotions, awareness, and value judgments. Different from the ears, eyes, nose, and mouth, which sense the outer world in a passive way, the heart is capable of thinking and performing intellectual and moral evaluations on the basis of analyzing and sorting out what these organs have sensed. Mencius believed that the heart consists of four aspects: compassion, deference, sense of shame or detestation, and conscience. Preserving and expanding one's good heart is the central aim in practicing moral teachings. According to Daoism, a serene and uncluttered heart is the highest state for a human being, much like a peaceful pool of still water. Such calmness is the way in which the heart can capture the essence of all things in the world.

CITATIONS

The sensory organs like ears and eyes cannot think. Therefore, they tend to be overwhelmed by the representation of external objects, and be led astray by those objects when coming into contact with them. The heart, however, is an organ capable of thinking. Thinking yields insight, while lack of it will get one nowhere. (*Mencius*)

Heart is the dominant organ of one's body. (*Classified Conversations of Master Zhu Xi*)

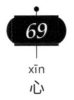

70

xìn yán bù měi, měi yán bù xìn
信言不美，美言不信

Trustworthy Words May Not Be Fine-sounding; Fine-sounding Words May Not Be Trustworthy.

To address the extravagance in social mores and in the style of writing of his time, Laozi advocated simple and natural lifestyles and literary presentations. During the Wei and Jin dynasties, men of letters valued natural and simple literary styles and were opposed to extravagant and superficial styles. This line of thought led to the emergence of great poets like Tao Yuanming, and shaped literary writings to reflect direct thoughts and natural expressions. Subsequently, ancient Chinese literature and art took simplicity and naturalness as the highest aesthetic standards.

CITATIONS

Trustworthy words may not be fine-sounding; fine-sounding words may not be trustworthy. A kind-hearted person may not be an eloquent speaker; a glib person is often not kind. (*Laozi*)

Laozi detested pretense, so he said, "Flower y rhetoric words may not be trustworthy." However, the 5,000-word *Dao De Jing* (another name of *Laozi*) he wrote is not only profound in ideas but reads beautifully. That means he was not opposed to writings using fine words. (Liu Xie: *The Literary Mind and the Carving of Dragons*)

71

xīngguānqúnyuàn
兴观群怨

Stimulation, Contemplation, Communication, and Criticism

According to Confucius, *The Book of Songs* served these four purposes, which summarize the basic functions and values of literature. "Stimulation" means that the appreciation of literary works arouses imagination, stimulates reflection on society and life, and inspires aspirations and interests. "Contemplation" means that reading leads to understanding nature, society, life, and politics. "Communication" means that reading encourages discussion with others, and exchange of thoughts and feelings. "Criticism" means learning how to critically express oneself about state affairs and voice inner feelings. These four functions are closely associated and involve the aesthetic, cognitive, and educational functions of literature. Later scholars have continued to make original contributions to the study of these themes.

CITATIONS

The Book of Songs stimulates the mind, inspires contemplation, enables one to understand society, exchange feelings and thoughts with others, and express resentment. The book guides one on how to support and wait on one's parents at home and how to serve one's sovereign in public life. One can also learn about birds, beasts, and plants from the book. (*The Analects*)

If works created on the basis of the author's understanding have the value of cognition, his understanding must have been profound. If his feelings are based on recognition, his observation must have been sharp. If certain resentment arises from discussions among a group of people, it must be unforgettable. If a group of people have come together because they share certain resentment, they must be closely knit. (Wang Fuzhi: *Desultory Remarks on Poetry from Ginger Studio*)

72

xīngxiàng

兴象

Xingxiang (Inspiring Imagery)

Inspiring imagery is an artistic achievement of profound literary significance and with great aesthetic taste, obtained through the perfect blending of an author's feelings with an objective situation or scenery. *Xing* (兴) is an impromptu inspiration of the author, and *xiang* (象) a material object he borrows from the external world in his writing. Tang- dynasty poetry critic Yin Fan first used the term "inspiring imagery" in his "Preface to *A Collection of Poems by Distinguished Poets*" in commenting on the works of poets in the golden period of the Tang Dynasty. It later became a standard for assessing the merit of a poetic work.

CITATIONS

These poets' works feature both inspiring imagery, as well as *fenggu* (class and integrity). (Yin Fan: Preface to *A Collection of Poems by Distinguished Poets*)

Poetry has two basic aspects: one includes form, rhythm, and rhyme; the other includes imagery and charm. (Hu Yinglin: *An In-Depth Exploration of Poetry*)

73

xìng

性

Xing (Nature)

Xing (性) mainly referred to human nature in ancient times. The concept of *xing* has two essential points. First, it refers to the inherent nature of all things, not as a result of nurture. Second, it refers to the common nature of certain kind of things, not the nature of individual things of that kind. Similarly, human nature, too, has two meanings. First, it refers to inherent attributes all people share, including physical features, desires, and consciousness. Second, it is the essential and distinct attribute that distinguishes people from birds and beasts, in other words, human's moral nature. Scholars throughout history held varied views over the question whether human nature was good or evil. Some believed it was good. Some thought it was evil. Some held that it was neither good nor evil. Some held that human nature could be both good and evil in the same person. Some thought that human nature was good in some people, but evil in others.

CITATIONS

To love food and good looks is but human nature. (*Mencius*)

Human nature is in line with the principles of heaven. (*Writings of the Cheng Brothers*)

74

xìnglíng
性灵

Xingling (Inner Self)

The term refers to an individual's inner mind vis-à-vis the outside world, which consists of two aspects, namely, temperament and talent. During the Southern and Northern Dynasties, *xingling* (inner self) became widely used in literary writing and criticism. It refers to the combination of a writer's temperament and talent, other than his social ethics, political beliefs, and literary traditions; and it stresses that literature is inspired by traits of individuality and should give expression to them. During the Ming and Qing dynasties, along with the trend of giving free rein to individuality and shaking off intellectual straitjacket, renowned scholars such as Yuan Hongdao and Yuan Mei advocated giving full expression to one's inner self, namely, one's thoughts, sentiment, emotion and views. They underscored the role of intellectual and artistic individuality in literary creation as opposed to the rigid School of Principle of the earlier Song and Ming dynasties, literary dogma and blind belief in classicism which constrained people from expressing human nature and inhabited literary creativity. The Xingling School thus became an important school in literary creation.

CITATIONS

Temperament and talent are found only in man, constituting his inner self. One of the three essential forms of existence along with heaven and earth, man stands out among all species and is the essence and soul of the world. In the natural course of events, the need to express man's inner self leads to the emergence of language, which in turn gives rise to literary creation. (Liu Xie: *The Literary Mind and the Carving of Dragons*)

Most of my brother Xiaoxiu's poems express his inner self, without being constrained by the rigid patterns and structures of ancient literary writings. He would not commit to paper anything not flowing naturally from his inner world. (Yuan Hongdao: Preface to Xiaoxiu's Poetry)

Ever since *The Book of Songs* was written, all those poems which have remained popular were created to give full expression to the authors' inner self, instead of being loaded with clichés and classical references. (Yuan Mei: *Suiyuan Poetry*)

75

xiūqízhìpíng

修齐治平

Self-cultivation, Family Regulation, State Governance, Bringing Peace to All Under Heaven

Self-cultivation is the starting point of several steps moving outward. The next step is managing family affairs, followed by governing the state. The final step is moving to provide peace and sound governance to all under heaven. This process is a fundamental theme in Confucian moral philosophy and discourse on politics. It is a gradually expanding process beginning with the individual and emanating outward into serving and benefiting an ever-larger whole. In such a process an individual's virtue and self-improvement are inseparable from his political aspirations.

CITATION

The ancients, who wished to promote illustrious virtue under heaven, first had to rule their own states well. Wishing to govern their states well, they first had to manage their fiefdoms well. Wishing to manage their fiefdoms well, they first had to cultivate themselves. (*The Book of Rites*)

76

xū

虚

Xu

Xu refers to a state of the cosmos or a state of mind. Basically, it has two different meanings. The first refers to the origin of the universe, indicating that everything originates from *xu*. Different ancient thinkers have different interpretations of this notion: Some take *xu* as being devoid of anything; others believe it is the state of existence of *qi* (气). Because *qi* is invisible and formless, it is said to be empty, but not a vacuum totally devoid of anything. The second meaning of *xu* refers to a state of mind that is peaceful, not preoccupied or simply free of any preconceptions.

CITATIONS

Xu is formless; it is the original state of *qi*. (Zhang Zai: *Enlightenment Through Confucian Teachings*)

Dao gathers and presents itself in an unoccupied and peaceful mind; being unoccupied means the pure state of the mind. (*Zhuangzi*)

77

xūjìng
虚静

Void and Peace

Void and peace mean that all distractions, such as desires and rational thoughts, should be dispelled to attain peace and purity of the soul. The idea of void and peace was first proposed by Laozi and Zhuangzi, the founders of Daoism, and then used by Xunzi to refer to a state of mental concentration. Such a state of mind is similar to the psychological conditions in appreciation of works of literature and art, which are characterized by being totally free from the awareness of oneself and the outside world, and free from any urge and desire. Therefore, thinkers and literary critics of earlier times used this term to explain the state of mind in literary and artistic creation and appreciation. It stressed the need for spiritual freedom in artistic creation, suggesting that this is an important precondition for reaching the highest level of aesthetic appreciation.

CITATIONS

When one attains the state of void and peace, his mind becomes peaceful and free of any distractions. He can withstand the temptations of the outside world. (*Laozi*)

In conceiving an essay, one should strive for a mental state of quiet emptiness and not let oneself be bothered by external interferences, and be relaxed and at ease just like all his internal organs are put in perfect comfort and his spirits refreshed by a thorough wash. (Liu Xie: *The Literary Mind and the Carving of Dragons*)

78

xuánlǎn
玄览

Xuanlan (Pure-minded Contemplation)

This term was first used by Laozi as a way to understand Dao. He believed that one cannot understand Dao by calmly observing everything unless one abandons all distracting thoughts and biases, and keeps one's mind as clear as a mirror. Later literary critics believed that the state of mind as required for *xuanlan* has similarities with the state of mind required for literary writing and appreciation, thus they made it an important term to mean one's state of mind must transcend all desires and personal gains in literary writing and appreciation.

CITATIONS

Is it for sure that there will be no flaws when one cleanses away all distracting thoughts and watches the world with a clear, peaceful mind? (*Laozi*)

Standing between heaven and earth and watching the world with a clear, peaceful mind, the writer enriches and improves himself through reading great works of the past. (Lu Ji: The Art of Writing)

79

xuǎnjǔ

选举

Select and Recommend

This term refers to the traditional way through which men were selected and appointed to government offices. Designed to achieve an ideal state of rule, the method worked to select and recommend people with outstanding virtue and talent into the system of political power and put them to official posts, where they took charge of the governance of the country. Although the mechanism varied from dynasty to dynasty, it always emphasized a person's moral integrity, ability, wisdom, and family background. It basically ensured that social elites had vertical mobility in the system of political power, and reflected the concepts of "rule of man" and "rule of virtue."

CITATION

Officials were chosen mainly through four channels: recommendations by government-run schools, imperial civil examinations, recommendations, and selection according to ability. Schools trained talent, imperial civil examinations recruited talent, recommendations served as a supplementary means to seek talent, and the Ministry of Civil Appointment selected officials according to their ability. In this way, all talent in the country could be recruited. (*The History of the Ming Dynasty*)

80

yǎsú

雅俗

Highbrow and Lowbrow

Highbrow and lowbrow, a dichotomy in literary criticism, refer to two kinds of literary and artistic works, namely, the refined versus the popular, and the lofty versus the vulgar. Highbrow describes works that are elegant and reflect what conforms with mainstream ideology, whereas lowbrow-art forms tend to meet popular aesthetic standard. From the perspective of art creation, highbrow art may be exquisite, but often appears affected, whereas lowbrow art, which has a folk origin, is natural, refreshing, unaffected, and unconstrained. From the Tang Dynasty onward, it became a trend for men of letters to borrow the best from popular art, thus further spurring the growth of lowbrow art, enriching cultural life and leading to more diversified artistic expressions.

CITATIONS

Confucius said, "I detest replacing red with purple and interfering refined classical music with the music of the State of Zheng. I loathe those who overthrow the state with their glib tongues." (*The Analects*)

The art of painting requires masterful use of colors, while the art of writing entails effective expression of thoughts and emotions. One needs to blend different colors in order to depict the different shapes of dogs and horses. Only writings that integrate thoughts and emotions demonstrate their highbrow or lowbrow qualities. (Liu Xie: *The Literary Mind and the Carving of Dragons*)

81

yǎngqì

养气

Cultivating *Qi*

This term suggests cultivating one's moral spirit and improving one's physical and mental well-being to achieve the best state of mind during literary creation in order to write excellent works. "Cultivating *qi* (气)" has three implications: 1) in the pre-Qin period Mencius emphasized that the virtuous and the capable should foster a "righteous *qi*" conducive to moral cultivation; 2) *A Comparative Study of Different Schools of Learning* by Wang Chong of the Eastern Han Dynasty has a chapter entitled "Treatise on Cultivating *Qi*," which emphasizes *qi* cultivation primarily in regards to maintaining good health; 3) Liu Xie of the Southern Dynasties, in *The Literary Mind and the Carving of Dragons,* drew upon the foregoing ideas and suggested maintaining good physical condition and a free, composed mental state in the initial phase of literary creation, while opposing excessive mental exertion. "Cultivating *qi*" subsequently became an important term in the lexicon of literary psychology.

CITATIONS

I am capable of differentiating between the thoughts and sentiments people convey in their words because I know how to cultivate my *qi,* and keep it strong. (*Mencius*)

Hence, when engaging in writing one must learn how to constrain and regulate oneself, keep one's mind pure and peaceful, and modulate one's mental vitality and activities. One should stop writing when upset so as not to disrupt one's train of thinking. (Liu Xie: *The Literary Mind and the Carving of Dragons*)

82

yī

一

The One

The term has three meanings. First, it indicates the original essence of all things. It is another name for *dao* (way). It is also referred to as *taiyi* (the supreme one). Second, it refers to the state of chaos before the separation of heaven and earth. The one was divided and transformed into heaven and earth. All things in heaven and on earth were produced from this Chaotic entity. Third, it indicates the unity of things, as opposed to "many" or "two." The idea is to emphasize the unity among things which are different or opposite.

CITATIONS

The one is the origin of everything. (Dong Zhongshu: Replies to the Emperor's Questions After Being Recommended)

Unity cannot be seen without the contradiction between two opposite sides, while the two opposite sides cannot exist without unity. (Zhang Zai: *Enlightenment Through Confucian Teachings*)

83

yì

义

Righteousness

The basic meaning of *yi* (义) is "reasonable" and "proper." It has two extended meanings. One is the proper basis and standard for people's actions. The other is to adjust one's words or deeds to meet certain standards, under the guidance of moral judgments. Scholars in the Song Dynasty used *li* (理) or "principles of heaven" to interpret *yi*, and considered *yi* to be the reasonable standard defined by the "principles of heaven," and hoped that people's words and deeds would fall in line with the "principles of heaven."

CITATIONS

A man of virtue understands and does what is morally right. (*The Analects*)

Righteousness means exercising self-restraint in order to do everything properly. (Zhu Xi: *Mencius Variorum*)

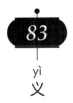

84

yìxiàng
意象

Yixiang (Imagery)

Imagery refers to a typical image in literary works, which embodies the author's subjective feelings and unique artistic conceptions. *Yi* (意) literally means an author's feelings and thoughts, and *xiang* (象) refers to the image of a material object in the external world, an artistic image reflecting the author's thoughts and feelings. In literary creation, imagery often refers to those images in nature with which an author's feelings and thoughts are associated. Emphasizing the harmonious relationship between beauty in both form and content, it is a mature state of literary creation.

CITATIONS

An author explores the imagery in his mind, conceives a work, and writes it down. (Liu Xie: *The Literary Mind and the Carving of Dragons*)

What a wonderful state of nature it is when the imagery of a poem is about to emerge! (Sikong Tu: Twenty-Four Styles of Poetry)

85

yīnyáng

阴阳

Yin and Yang

The primary meaning of yin and yang is the orientation of things in relation to the sun, with yang meaning the sunny side and yin the shady side. There are two extended meanings: 1) two opposite kinds of *qi* (气) in nature; and 2) two basic contrary forces or qualities that coexist, thus the active, hot, upward, outward, bright, forward, and strong are yang, while the passive, cold, downward, inward, dark, backward, and weak are yin. The interaction between yin and yang, or yin *qi* and yang *qi*, determines the formation and existence of all things. The theory of yin and yang later became the basis for ancient Chinese to explain and understand the universe and everything in it, social order, and human relations. For example, heaven is yang and earth is yin, ruler is yang and subordinates are yin, husband is yang and wife is yin, noble is yang and ignoble is yin, leading is yang and following is yin.

CITATIONS

All things stand, facing yang and against yin. The interaction between yin and yang creates a state of harmony. (*Laozi*)

Yin and yang cannot work without each other. (Dong Zhongshu: *Luxuriant Gems of The Spring and Autumn Annals*)

86

yǐnxiù

隐秀

Latent Sentiment and Evident Beauty

This term means that prose and poetry may contain latent sentiments and thoughts, as well as expressions and sentences that present an apparent sense of beauty. "Latent sentiment and evident beauty" first appeared as the title of a chapter in *The Literary Mind and the Carving of Dragons*. There, "latent sentiment" means what lies beyond events and landscapes in a narrative or a description, triggering imaginations on the part of the reader. On the other hand, "evident beauty" refers to the kind of beauty created by expressions and sentences in a piece of writing, which bring out that latent meaning. The latent and the apparent qualities are inseparable, constituting an aesthetic feature of good literary works. Later, this term developed into a rhetorical device in writing prose and poetry.

CITATIONS

Thus, an excellent piece of writing should have both beautiful in language and a message hidden between the lines. The former refers to beautiful sentences and expressions that accentuate the message of the writing while the latter represents the multiple significance that lies beyond the text. (Liu Xie: *The Literary Mind and the Carving of Dragons*)

Latency happens when feelings and thoughts are hidden between the lines of a literary work. Evident beauty occurs when messages of sentiment and feelings are vividly portrayed by the images the author creates. (Zhang Jie: *Notes on Poetry Written in the Pine and Cypress Studio*)

87

yǒu dé zhě bì yǒu yán
有德者必有言

Virtuous People Are Sure to Produce Fine Writing.

Virtuous people are sure to write fine works which will be passed on to later generations. According to Confucianism, the moral character of a writer determines the value of his work, virtuous people would naturally write well, but those who wrote well might not necessarily be virtuous. Therefore, authors should write to disseminate moral values; virtue and writings should be consistent. However, later Confucian scholars sometimes overemphasized the influence that ethics and the authors' moral character had on their writings to the neglect of the characteristics and values of literary creation per se.

CITATIONS

Confucius said, "Virtuous people are sure to have good writings or words to pass on to later generations, but it is not always true the other way round." (*The Analects*)

A man of character should possess exceptional capability and his eloquent expressions should portray everything truthfully. His great wisdom should enable him to explain all things under heaven. He does not need to hide his aspirations to serve as a model of virtue. If he has come to a good understanding of Dao, he surely will disseminate it extensively. (Liu Xie: *The Literary Mind and the Carving of Dragons*)

88

yǒujiào-wúlèi
有教无类

Education for All Without Discrimination

Education can and must be provided for all. It eliminates the differences in social status and wealth. (Another explanation is that education should be provided to students without discrimination on the basis of social status or wealth.) Education consists of teaching of social norms, music, and moral principles. A non-discriminatory approach to education means making no distinction between students based on their social status, wealth, mental capability, moral character, geographic location, or ethnicity. Transcending differences in social status, geography, and ethnicity, education for all without discrimination is a humanistic ideal that champions equal treatment of all people and rejects all forms of discrimination.

CITATION

The moral values promoted by ancient sages are universal. That is why "once the same education is provided, differences in geography and ethnicity would be smoothed out." When the Tujue people who suffered from war trauma and were in predicament submitted themselves to the Tang Dynasty, we should assist and protect them, let them settle down among us, teach them social norms and law, and help them engage in farming... What should we be worried about? (*The New Tang History*)

89

yǒuwú

有无

You and *Wu*

The term has three definitions. First, it describes two different dimensions of things: One is with form and the other without form. Second, it refers to two different stages or states of a thing during its generation, existence, and demise. *You* (有) refers to the state of a thing after it has come into being and before it dies out; *wu* (无) refers to the state of a thing before its birth and after its death. Third, *you* refers to any tangible or identifiable thing or the sum total of such things; *wu* refers to the original source or ontological existence, which is intangible and unidentifiable, and transcends all specific objects. With regard to the third definition, some philosophers consider *wu* to be the original source or ontological existence of the world, and *you* comes from *wu*; others believe that *you* is fundamentally significant, and dispute the notion that *you* owes its existence to *wu*. Despite their differences, *you* and *wu* are mutually dependent.

CITATIONS

Therefore, the with-form part of an object provides ease and convenience, whereas the without-form part performs the functions of that object. (*Laozi*)

The formation and existence of *you* originate from *wu*. (Wang Bi: *Annotations on Laozi*)

90

yuánqǐ
缘起

Dependent Origination

The term is a translation of the Sanskrit word *pratītyasamutpāda*. *Yuan* (缘) means conditions; *qi* (起) means origination. That is to say, all things, phenomena, and social activities arise out of the combinations of causes and conditions. They exist in the continuous relationship between causes and conditions. Thus all things originate, change, and demise depending upon certain conditions. Dependent origination is the fountainhead of Buddhist thought and forms the common theoretical basis for all Buddhist schools and sects. Buddhism uses this concept to explain everything in the universe, the constant changes of social and spiritual phenomena, and the internal laws of origination, change, and demise.

CITATION

All things originate out of the combinations of causes and conditions, thus they cannot be regarded as original existence; at the same time, they arise, change, and demise upon certain conditions, so they cannot be said as non-existence. (Sengzhao: *Treatises of Sengzhao*)

91

zhīyīn
知音

Resonance and Empathy

The term is about appreciating and understanding the ideas in literary and artistic works and the thoughts of their authors. The original meaning was feeling a sense of resonance with music. It was later extended by literary critics in the Wei, Jin, and Southern and Northern dynasties to mean resonance or empathy between writers / artists and their readers / viewers. As a core concept in literary criticism, it touches upon both general and particular issues in artistic creation and appreciation, involves rich intellectual implications, and meshes with the audience's response in Western criticism, receptive aesthetics, and hermeneutics.

CITATIONS

Talking about melody with someone who has no ear for natural sounds would be a waste of time, and so would discussing music with someone who knows nothing about melody. One who knows music is close to understanding social norms. (*The Book of Rites*)

It is such a challenge to understand music! Since music is so hard to understand, it is difficult to find people who can appreciate it. It may take a thousand years to find someone who understands music! (Liu Xie: *The Literary Mind and the Carving of Dragons*)

92

zhíxún
直寻

Direct Quest

A poet should directly express his thoughts and sentiments when he is inspired. This is a concept for writing poems proposed by poetry critic Zhong Rong of the Southern Dynasties in his work "The Critique of Poetry" as a reaction to the excessive use of allusions and quotes from earlier works. Inspired by naturalist ideas of Daoism and by his own reading of the fine works of earlier poets, he developed a new form of poetic creation which he named "direct quest." By this, he meant directly describing matters that one senses and learns about, directly expressing one's inner feelings, and creating aesthetic images in which the sensibilities match up with current realities. The theory of natural disposition and intelligence used in Ming- and Qing-dynasty poetics was influenced by this idea.

CITATIONS

A comprehensive survey of the best-known works of ancient and current poets shows that most of the poets did not borrow favored lines or literary allusions from their predecessors, but directly sought inspirations from their personal experiences. (Zhong Rong: Preface to "The Critique of Poetry")

Since I want to use my own words to express my feelings, how can I let myself be bound by the content and forms of ancient writings? (Huang Zunxian: Five Poems on Random Thoughts)

93

zhōngguó

中国

Zhongguo (China)

This term refers to the areas along the middle and lower reaches of the Yellow River where ancient Huaxia (华夏) people or the Han people lived. Originally, the term Zhongguo (中国) meant both this region and its culture. The Huaxia people established their states along the Yellow River. Believing the areas were located in the center of the world, they called it Zhongguo (the Central Country, as against other areas around it). Later, the term was used to refer to the Central Plains in North China and the states founded in that area. Since the Qing Dynasty, Zhongguo has been used to refer specifically to all the territory of China and its sovereignty. Currently, Zhongguo is used as the abbreviated form of the People's Republic of China.

CITATIONS

Give benefit to the people in the capital, and reassure and pacify all the feudal dukes and princes in the country. (*The Book of Songs*)

If the areas of Wu and Yue (under the control of Sun Quan) could stand up to confront the central region (under the control of Cao Cao), the former should better cut ties with the latter. (*The History of the Three Kingdoms*)

94

zhōnghuá
中华

Zhonghua

This term is an abbreviation of the compound word formed by Zhongguo (中国) and Huaxia (华夏). Here, *hua* (华) also means "flower" or "flowery," which was used as an analogy for a splendid culture. The ancestors of the Huaxia people established their state in the middle and lower reaches of the Yellow River, which they thought was the center (*zhong*) of the world and which had a flourishing culture (*hua*), so the state was called Zhonghua. This multi-ethnic state, with the Huaxia people as the predominant group of its population, later began its territorial expansions, and the places where it extended to became part of Zhonghua. In modern times, Zhonghua became a term denoting China, the Chinese people, and its culture.

CITATION

Zhonghua refers to China. Under the wise rule of the sage king, all his subjects belong to China. They are dressed in a dignified manner, practice filial piety, love and respect the elderly, and follow moral norms in personal and social conduct. This is the country called Zhonghua. (*Commentary and Explanation on Well-Known Law Cases of the Tang Dynasty*)

95

zhōngyōng
中庸

Zhongyong (Golden Mean)

Zhongyong (golden mean) was considered to be the highest level of virtue by Confucius and Confucian scholars. *Zhong* (中) means moderate in one's words and deeds. Everything has its limits, and neither exceeding nor falling short of the limits is desirable. *Yong* (庸) has two meanings. One is common or ordinary and the other is unchanging. Moderation can be maintained for over a long time only when one practices it in everyday life. *Zhongyong* means the standard of moderation that one should follow in dealing with others and in one's everyday conduct.

CITATIONS

Zhongyong is the highest of virtues. (*The Analects*)

Zhongyong does not bend one way or the other; it is the common principle of neither exceeding nor falling short of the line. (Zhu Xi: *Commentary on The Doctrine of the Mean*)

96

zīwèi

滋味

Nuanced Flavor

This term refers to an effect that allows lasting satisfaction and rewarding in poetry appreciation, which is a particular sense of beauty offered by poetry. In the Southern Dynasties, poetry critic Zhong Rong proposed in "The Critique of Poetry" that in writing five-character-per-line poems, one should pay special attention to the combination of form and content, so that readers could enjoy a poem with inexhaustible delight. Later, nuanced flavor also came to refer to a kind of taste in literary and artistic creation.

CITATIONS

Five-character-per-line poems constitute the most important poetic form and are most richly imbued with nuanced flavors. (Zhong Rong: Preface to "The Critique of Poetry")

A literary work cultivates the mind, implicitly satirizes or criticizes a monarch, and enables the reader to obtain a sense of aesthetic appreciation. Reading such works gives one great delight. (Yan Zhitui: *Admonitions for the Yan Clan*)

97

zǐ zhī duó zhū
紫之夺朱

Purple Prevailing over Red

This refers to evil prevailing over good and falsehood being mistaken for truth in literature and art as well as in social life. It is red, not purple, that was viewed as a truly proper color by the ancient Chinese. Confucius, upset by the loss of judgment over good and evil, and by the fact that vulgar music was taking the place of refined classical music in the Spring and Autumn Period, called for dispelling confusion and putting things in the right order. With this in mind, Liu Xie of the Southern Dynasties criticized some writers for abandoning Confucian teachings and catering to vulgar tastes. Scholars of later generations used this notion to reaffirm Confucian criteria and norms for literary creation.

CITATIONS

Confucius said, "I detest replacing red with purple and interfering refined classical music with the music of the State of Zheng. I loathe those who overthrow the state with their glib tongues." (*The Analects*)

Rhetoric is like the skin of an essay; the writer's thoughts and feelings are its marrow. A piece of elegant writing is like the embroidery on a ceremonial gown in ancient times – magnificent and dignified. Excessive focus on rhetoric and technique, however, is no different from an abnormal color taking the place of a truly proper one. (Liu Xie: *The Literary Mind and the Carving of Dragons*)

98

zìrán

自然

Naturalness

The term refers to the primordial state of things, unaffected by the various meanings imposed on it by man. The concept of naturalness in philosophy is different from that of nature in the ordinary sense. In daily language, the term refers to the physical world, which is independent of human interference, as opposed to human society. In philosophy, there is also a natural state of man and society. In political philosophy, "naturalness" specifically applies to the natural state enjoyed by ordinary people free from the intervention of government supervision and moral edification. Daoism holds that in governance a monarch should conform to the natural state of the people.

CITATIONS

Dao takes naturalness as its law. (*Laozi*)

Heaven and earth allow everything to follow their natural course without imposing any interference so that all things interact and govern themselves. (Wang Bi: *Annotations on Laozi*)

99

zìrán yīngzhǐ
自然英旨

Charm of Spontaneity

This term means poetry creation should present the unembellished beauty of nature and the genuine sentiments of human beings. The original meaning of *yingzhi* (英旨) is good taste. Used as a literary term, however, it refers to charming content and imagery in poetry. In "Preface to 'The Critique of Poetry,'" Zhong Rong of the Southern Dynasties called on poets to express their thoughts and sentiments in their own words and opposed borrowing expressions from ancient poets. He criticized the excessive attention to ornate language and tonal rhythms in the writing of five-character-per-line poetry. He maintained that spontaneously created poems of good taste were most valuable. The expressions "natural" and "simple and unaffected" in later literary criticisms contain Zhong Rong's ideas.

CITATIONS

Ren Fang, Wang Rong and some other writers of recent times have given no attention to linguistic innovation yet vied with each other for using literary allusions that no one else has ever employed. Subsequent writers have turned this practice into a habit. And so, all sentences must contain allusions, and every word and expression has to be traceable to some sources. Allusions are clumsily tacked onto the authors' own words, severely damaging their works. There are few poets capable of producing works that display the pristine beauty of nature or their genuine sentiments. (Zhong Rong: Preface to "The Critique of Poetry")

I have read with great interest the letters, poems, and essays you have sent to me. Broadly speaking, they are all like floating clouds and flowing waters, have no set form or structure, and frequently flow when they should flow and remain still when they must stop. The articles are presented in a natural way and have multiple and uninhibited styles. (Su Shi: A Letter of Reply to Xie Minshi)

100

zōngfǎ

宗法

Feudal Clan System

This system was central to life in ancient China; it was a system of principles and measures by which a clan, a state, or society was run, based on bloodline or whether a son was born from the wife or a concubine. The feudal clan system evolved from the patriarchal chiefs system. Taking shape during the Western Zhou Dynasty, this system and the feudal system were mutually dependent and complementary. The feudal clan system had two levels: one was the familial level, where the eldest son by the wife was the first in line to inherit the family's property and thus enjoyed the greatest authority. Other members of the clan were allotted their status and authority according to their closeness of kinship, ancestry, or seniority. In the families of the emperor, kings, and other nobility, this pattern was extended to the state or national level. It had a decisive impact on the inheritance of the imperial throne and on state politics. The feudal clan system greatly influenced the Chinese way of life and thinking for several thousand years.

CITATION

The feudal clan system is a state's bedrock for fostering and educating its people. (Feng Guifen: *My Argument for Restoring the Feudal Clan System*)

PART II

101

āntǔ-zhòngqiān
安土重迁

Attached to the Land and Unwilling to Move

Feeling attached to the native land and reluctant to move to another place. This was a widespread way of thinking and sentiment among the common people in a traditional agricultural society. In essence, it is because they depended on the land to make a living, since the land served as their basic resource for production and livelihood. Also, they were loath to leave the burial place of their ancestors as well as their family and relations. In the Chinese clan system, ancestor worship was a basic belief and living together with one's clan was the social norm. People felt it upsetting and inconvenient to leave the environment and society in which they grew up. This concept and sentiment may seem passive and conservative, but it reflects the Chinese people's simple love for their homeland, relatives, and a peaceful life.

CITATION

Attached to the land and unwilling to move – this is the nature of the common people. Interdependent among relatives and reluctant to leave them – this is a shared feeling. (*The History of the Han Dynasty*)

102

bāguà

八卦

Eight Trigrams

Each of the eight trigrams consists of three lines and each line is either divided (– –) or undivided (—), representing yin or yang respectively. The eight trigrams are: *qian* (☰), *kun* (☷), *zhen* (☳), *xun* (☴), *kan* (☵), *li* (☲), *gen* (☶), and *dui* (☱). According to the ancient Chinese, the eight trigrams symbolized basic things and phenomena of nature or society and represented heaven, earth, thunder, wind, water, fire, mountain, and lake respectively. The ancient Chinese also used the interchanges and transformations of the eight trigrams and what they represented to understand and expound on natural and social changes and to explain why and how they took place.

CITATION

When Fuxi was the ruler under heaven, he looked up into the sky to observe celestial phenomena and looked down on the land to observe geographical features and examine the images of birds, animals, and all other things that existed on earth. He selected symbols from the human body close by and from various objects far away, and then invented the eight trigrams to explain the miraculous nature and distinguish the states of all things. (*The Book of Changes*)

103

bĕnsè
本色

Bense (Original Character)

The term originally referred to true colors and has been extended to mean true appearance. As a term of literary critique, *bense* (本色) has three meanings: 1) the artistic style and literary features that are compatible with a given genre; 2) the style and literary features that remain true to the writer's individual character; and 3) the style that makes it possible for the writing to remain true to the author's own experience and that gives truthful expression to his thoughts and feelings. *Bense* is not only a requirement for the writer but also for his works. In the literary criticism of the Song Dynasty, *bense* was often used to describe and evaluate the special qualities of different genres. In the literary criticism of the Ming and Qing dynasties, *bense* usually referred to the individual style of poets and writers and also those styles of writing that remained true to life experience and eschewed literary embellishment. *Bense* is often used together with *danghang* (当行) to mean "original and genuine"; it is often associated with the Dao of nature in classical Daoist philosophy, in opposition to the attitude and styles that stress literary embellishment.

CITATIONS

Poems written by Han Yu read like essays and *ci* lyrics by Su Shi read like poems. This is like Master Dancer Lei of the Song Palace Music School performing dances choreographed for women. Although they were good writers, what they wrote was incompatible with the original characters of the genres. (Chen Shidao: *Houshan's Understanding of Poetry*)

Recently I have come to realize that in writing poetry or prose, all that is needed is to write what I have in mind. This is like the Chinese saying, "When you open the mouth, others can see your throat." When readers read such works, they will come to know what the author is actually like. Without hiding either strengths or weaknesses, the author makes his true character fully apparent. The writing that best embodies the author's original character is most desirable. (Tang Shunzhi: Letter to Hong Fangzhou)

Everything in the world has its true appearance and its surrogate. True appearance is what I am, while a surrogate is a substitute. (Xu Wei: Foreword to *Romance of the West Chamber*)

104

bǐdé

比德

Virtue Comparison

The term means likening certain characteristics of things in nature, including plants and animals, to human virtues. When extended to the domain of literary appreciation, it generally involves likening desirable objects to a noble personality. To perceive a natural phenomenon as a reflection or symbol of human characteristics is typical of the Confucian School, which takes aesthetic quality as a moral standard for people as well as literature and arts. Likening humans to nature implies that appreciation of nature is actually appreciation of humanity itself, particularly its moral character. It later became a technique employed in rhetoric and poetry.

CITATIONS

In the past, the moral integrity of a man of virtue was likened to fine jade, which is smooth, mellow, and lustrous, an exact embodiment of benevolence. (*The Book of Rites*)

By the time Qu Yuan wrote "Ode to the Orange", both his sentiment and literary style had become highly refined. He used orange to draw analogy and convey a certain message before preceding to describe details. (Liu Xie: *The Literary Mind and the Carving of Dragons*)

105

biàntǐ

辨体

Style Differentiation

The term refers to the differentiation of the form and style of a literary work. It means that before putting words on paper, one needs to decide on the form and style appropriate to the thoughts and feelings to be expressed so as to produce a fine literary work with a high degree of harmony between form and content. In creating literary works, ancient scholars tended to decide on the style before writing. Literary critics in the Wei, Jin, and Southern and Northern dynasties discussed in detail the artistic features and rules of all literary styles and stressed that authors must choose an appropriate form or style to express their thoughts and sentiments and strictly follow the rules of the style, language form, and writing technique required by the chosen form or style. This, they believed, was the only way to create excellent literary works. Contrary to the term "style differentiation," the term *poti* (破体) or "breaking-down styles" refers to the integration of different styles or forms of literary works by breaking down their boundaries. Style differentiation sometimes refers to differentiating the form or style of a literary work in order to attain a lofty character and realm of literature.

CITATIONS

Since literary works express different ideas, temperaments, and tastes, the writing skills and techniques used should also differ in order to suit the content. It is the content of a literary work that determines its style, which in turn gives strength to the work. Such strength comes from writing in accordance with the style of the literary work. (Liu Xie: *The Literary Mind and the Carving of Dragons*)

When the poet starts to compose a poem, if his conception of the poem tends towards grandeur, then the aesthetic conception of the poem will be grand; if his conception of the poem is free and easy, so will the aesthetic conception of the poem be. (Jiaoran: *Poetic Styles*)

One should first decide on the style or form of an article, and then start writing by following the rules required by the chosen style or form for the article. (Zhang Taiyan: *Overview of Traditional Chinese Scholarly Learning*)

106

biécái-biéqù

别材别趣

Distinct Subject and Artistic Taste

Poetry should have its distinct subject and artistic taste. In the Northern Song Dynasty, inspired by Huang Tingjian, poets of the Jiangxi School used poetry as a means to express views on public issues. In doing so, they tended to overlook the use of inspiring and evocative language unique to poetic expression. In *Canglang's Criticism of Poetry,* literary critic Yan Yu of the Southern Song Dynasty expressed his dismay at this trend. He argued that poetry should have its distinctive subject and purpose and that poetry should express the poet's sentiment and emotion rather than piling book knowledge or showing off learning or presenting theories. The message of a poem should be expressed through its aesthetic depiction. The advocating of distinct subject and artistic taste by Yan Yu shows that by the time of the Southern Song Dynasty, literary critics had recognized the distinctive features of poetic expression and called for return to the creative style of poetry writing of the Tang Dynasty.

CITATIONS

Poetry has its distinct subject matter and is not about book learning. It also has distinct artistic taste and is not about presenting theories. (Yan Yu: *Canglang's Criticism of Poetry*)

During the 300 years of the Song Dynasty, a lot of people published collections of literary works, many of which contained poems dealing with different subject matters. In these poems, some authors showcased their arguments, while others paraded their learning or indulged in scholarly debate. Some published 1,000 poems, and others published even 10,000 poems; but most of them were merely rhymed essays that expounded Confucian classics or discussed current policies. They were just not poetry. (Liu Kezhuang: Preface to *A Collection of Zhuxi's Poems*)

107

biéjí

别集

Individual Collection

The term refers to a collection of works by an individual author, in contrast to an anthology which amalgamates the works of many writers. In the Western Han Dynasty, Liu Xin composed *Seven Categories*, one of the categories being "The Catalogue of *Shi* and *Fu*," which collects the literary works of 66 writers including Qu Yuan, Tang Le, and Song Yu. Organized by author, "The Catalogue of *Shi* and *Fu*" was regarded as the beginning of individual collections. Many more individual collections were compiled in the Eastern Han Dynasty, as exemplified by the 886 collections of writers from the Han through Wei and Jin to the Southern and Northern Dynasties, recorded in *The History of the Sui Dynasty*. Nearly every author had his own collection. Collections devoted to poetry were usually entitled collection of poems while those concerned with prose or both poetry and prose were entitled collection of writings. An individual collection might be entitled after the author's name, pen name, posthumous title, birth place, or residence. Containing all the major works of an author, an individual collection enables readers to learn about the author's aspirations and therefore provides a valuable source for the study of his ideas and literary achievements for later generations.

CITATION

What is known as *bieji* (别集) appeared in the Eastern Han Dynasty. Literary history since Qu Yuan witnessed an increasing number of creative writers with distinctive aspirations, preferences, literary features, and tastes. To examine the style, strength, as well as the spiritual world of a specific author, later generations put together all his works and called it *ji* (集) or collection. (*The History of the Sui Dynasty*)

108

chéng

城

Fortress / City

Cheng (城) is a city with walls surrounding it. The Chinese character for *cheng* originally referred to inner and outer city walls built of earth, with military defense and flood control functions. Usually, it was surrounded by a moat. In ancient times, the state capital of a monarch, the fief of a prince, and a manor estate granted by a monarch to a minister or a senior official all had a walled settlement as the center, hence the name *cheng*. The Chinese character for *cheng* is pronounced the same way as another character meaning accommodating. Here, *cheng* means having the capacity to accommodate people. The primary function of a *cheng* is to protect its residents. This is a concrete manifestation of the political notion that people are the foundation of the state.

CITATIONS

A fortress / city is a facility used to defend the people inside. (*Mozi*)

A fortress / city is for accommodating people. (Xu Shen: *Explanation of Script and Elucidation of Characters*)

A fortress / city is built to protect people. (*Guliang's Commentary on The Spring and Autumn Annals*)

109

chǔcí

楚辞

Chuci (Ode of Chu)

Chuci (楚辞) was a poetic genre first attributed to Qu Yuan. It later became the title for the first anthology of poetry depicting the culture in south China. *Chuci* was so named because it made use of Chu (now Hunan and Hubei provinces) dialect, accent, and local special genres to describe the unique landscape, histor y, and folklore of the State of Chu. The term *chuci* first appeared in the early Western Han Dynasty, and later Liu Xiang compiled a literary collection including 16 pieces written by Qu Yuan, Song Yu, Huainan Xiaoshan (a group of authors of the Western Han Dynasty), Dongfang Shuo, Yan Ji, Wang Bao, and Liu Xiang. When Wang Yi later compiled *Verses from the Odes of Chu*, he added a work of his own to the collection, making it an anthology of 17 works. Through its distinctive genre and unique cultural elements, *chuci* reflected the special culture of the Chu region in southern China. As a genre, *chuci* is characterized by profound emotions, wild imagination, and rich allusions to the remote historical mythology from the dawn of Chinese history. It demonstrates an innovative and distinctive literary genre and spirit, standing with *The Book of Songs* as twin literary pinnacles. Later generations called this genre *Chuci* Style or *Sao* Style (Flowery Style), and its research *chuci* studies.

CITATIONS

It can be ascertained that works by Qu Yuan and his contemporaries in the State of Chu borrowed literary elements from the classics of the past ages, but also blended some stylistic features from the Warring States Period. Though less outstanding than *The Book of Songs,* they were masterpieces in poetry. (Liu Xie: *The Literary Mind and the Carving of Dragons*)

Generally speaking, the literary works of Qu Yuan and Song Yu used Chu dialect and exploited Chu rhythm and tunes to depict the landscape and scenery in Chu, hence called *chuci,* or odes of Chu. (Huang Bosi: Preface to *Odes of Chu* [*Revised Edition*])

110

chúnwáng-chǐhán
唇亡齿寒

Once the Lips Are Gone, the Teeth Will Feel Cold.

When two things are interdependent, the fall of one will endanger the other. According to the early chronicle *Zuo's Commentary on The Spring and Autumn Annals*, when the State of Jin wanted to march through the State of Yu in order to attack Yu's neighbor, the State of Guo. Gongzhiqi, a minister of Yu, remonstrated with his ruler, saying, "Guo provides a protective shield for Yu. If Guo falls, Yu will soon follow. The relationship between Yu and Guo is like that between lips and teeth." This shows that since ancient times the Chinese nation has been keen to maintain friendly ties with neighboring countries. It represents pragmatic geopolitical thinking of maintaining amity with close neighbors.

CITATION

To the states of Qi and Chu, the State of Zhao serves as a protective shield, just like the lips protecting the teeth. Once the lips are gone, the teeth will feel cold. If Zhao is defeated by the State of Qin today, the same fate will befall Qi and Chu tomorrow. (*Records of the Historian*)

111

cídá

辞达

Expressiveness

The term means to put forth one's thoughts in a clear and concise way when speaking and writing. Confucius opposed excessive efforts in pursuit of extravagant writing styles. He stressed that writings need only to express one's ideas and feelings clearly and precisely, and he advocated a concept of aesthetics that valued the combination of elegance and simplicity. This concept was successively inherited and developed by Liu Xie, Han Yu, Su Shi, and others, resulting in a Chinese literary style that strives for natural and pithy expression as opposed to extravagant embellishment.

CITATIONS

Confucius said, "It's good enough if you express yourself clearly." (*The Analects*)

If one can write expressively, his potential to achieve literary grace is boundless. (Su Shi: A Letter of Reply to Xie Minshi)

112

dào fǎ zìrán

道法自然

Dao Operates Naturally.

Dao operates in accordance with natural conditions of all things. This idea first appeared in the book *Laozi,* according to which "natural" means the natural state of things. Dao creates and nurtures everything, yet it does not command anything. In political philosophy, the relationship between Dao and natural things implies that between the ruler and the people. The rulers should follow the natural requirements of Dao, which places limits on their power, and govern by means of non-interference to allow the people and affairs to take their own natural course.

CITATION

Man patterns himself on the operation of the earth; the earth patterns itself on the operation of heaven; heaven patterns itself on the operation of Dao; Dao patterns itself on what is natural. (*Laozi*)

113

dū

都

Metropolis

The term refers to the city in which a state ruler resided and conducted government affairs. The difference between a *du* (都) and a *yi* (邑) was that the former had an ancestral temple to enshrine the memorial tablets of ancestors and previous rulers while the latter did not. An ancestral temple used to be a place where rulers, the nobility, and senior officials made offerings to their ancestors. Therefore, an ancestral temple was a product of ancestral worshipping and a symbol of the patriarchal clan system. It is the defining structure of a *du*. During the Zhou Dynasty, the political center of all ducal states was called *du*. From the Qin and Han dynasties onward, *du* referred to the place where the emperor lived. Later, all cities large in scale and population were called *du*.

CITATIONS

All cities with ancestral temples to house the memorial tablets of ancestors and previous rulers are called *du* while those without are called *yi*. (*Zuo's Commentary on The Spring and Autumn Annals*)

When a city is called *du*, it is where the ruler of the land resides and where there is a large population. (Liu Xi: *Explanation of Terms*)

114

dúhuà

独化

Self-driven Development

The term indicates that all things in heaven and on earth do not depend on external forces. Rather, they take shape and change by themselves independently. It was put forward by Guo Xiang in his *Annotations on Zhuangzi*. Specifically, the term contains three meanings. Firstly, all things in heaven and on earth form and change naturally. Secondly, all things in heaven and on earth form and change independent of one another. Thirdly, all things in heaven and on earth form and change suddenly, without any reason or purpose. The concept of self-driven development denies the existence of a creator. At the same time, it also denies that one thing causes the occurrence and existence of another. However, according to this concept, all things in the universe, naturally formed, co-exist in harmony.

CITATION

All that which comes into existence on its own neither depends on external laws nor does it depend internally on itself. Without any reason it came into being by itself and remains independent. (Guo Xiang: *Annotations on Zhuangzi*)

115

fǎ bù ē guì
法不阿贵

The Law Does Not Favor the Rich and Powerful.

The law treats everybody equally, not favoring the rich and powerful. The Legalists in ancient China argued that there should be no distinction between noble and poor or close and distant people; punishment or reward should be meted out strictly in accordance with the law. They believed in fairness in enforcing the law and treating everyone as equal before the law. This belief has been championed through the ages and is a major source of the notion of rule of law.

CITATION

The law does not favor the rich and powerful, as the marking-line does not bend. What the law imposes, the wise cannot evade, nor can the brave defy. Punishment for wrongdoing does not spare senior officials, as rewards for good conduct do not bypass the common man. (*Hanfeizi*)

116

fēigōng

非攻

Denouncing Unjust Wars

Opposition to unjust warfare is one of the basic concepts in the Mohist School of thought. It regards immoral and aggressive wars as acutely harmful to society. Not only does the country being attacked suffer great damage, the people of the country that starts the war also suffer serious casualties and property losses. Therefore, Mohists held that unjust wars should be prohibited. They took specific measures to prevent aggressive wars between nations, and conducted research into defensive tactics and armaments.

CITATION

If one wishes to be humane and just and become a gentleman with high moral standards, he must both observe the way of the sage kings, and advance the interests of the state and the people. In order to achieve these goals, the principle of prohibiting unjust wars cannot be disregarded. (*Mozi*)

117

gānchéng

干城

Shield and Fortress / Dukes and Princes

The term originally referred to shield and fortress, but was later used to mean dukes and princes, and then defenders of a regime, theory or proposition. *Gan* (干) means shield, a defensive weapon in old days, while *cheng* (城) means inner and outer city walls or a fortress, a structure for defensive purposes. Dukes and princes were likened to *gancheng* (干城), in contrast with *chongcheng* (崇城), which means supreme city, referring to the Son of Heaven and indicating his supreme position. It is meant that dukes and princes, likened to shield and fortress, had the responsibilities to defend the Son of Heaven. Hence, dukes and princes must obey orders from the Son of Heaven. As it has evolved over time, the term generally referred to loyal and efficient defenders. Interestingly, it came to mean that not only people of lower ranks defend their superiors, but also people of high positions defend their subordinates.

CITATIONS

The Son of Heaven is referred to as *chongcheng,* indicating his supreme and noble status, while dukes and princes are referred to as *gancheng,* meaning that they must not act on their own but pledge their obedience to the Son of Heaven. (*Debates of the White Tiger Hall*)

The valiant warriors are defenders of dukes and princes. (*The Book of Songs*)

With good governance, dukes and princes become defenders and protectors of their people. (*Zuo's Commentary on The Spring and Autumn Annals*)

118

gāngróu

刚柔

Gang and *Rou*

Two opposing properties or qualities that objects and human beings possess. The term has three different meanings. First, when describing natural or manmade objects, *gang* (刚) means hard and *rou* (柔) means soft. Second, when describing human qualities, *gang* means strong and determined, while *rou* means gentle and modest. Third, when describing a style of governance or law enforcement, *gang* means strict and *rou* means lenient. *Gang* and *rou* are one of the manifestations of yin and yang. Their mutual opposition and accommodation are the basic causes of change, and they must achieve a certain balance within any object or action. Too much of either is inappropriate and dangerous.

CITATIONS

The laws governing the ways of heaven are yin and yang, those governing the ways of the earth are *rou* and *gang*, and those governing the ways of human society are benevolence and righteousness. (*The Book of Changes*)

Change occurs when *gang* and *rou* interact. (*The Book of Changes*)

119

géming
革命

Changing the Mandate / Revolution

The term means taking power from a ruler. *Ge* (革) means to change or remove. *Ming* (命) first referred to the mandate of Heaven and later came to mean a ruler's decrees and his mandate to rule. Changing the mandate usually involves replacing a ruler and a change of dynasty, in other words, overthrowing an old regime and establishing a new one. People in ancient China believed that a ruler's mandate to rule was ordained by Heaven and therefore any change of the mandate should in essence be carried out in response to the will of Heaven. However, change is a basic law of the universe, and the removal of a ruler's mandate is a specific expression of this law. The legitimacy and success of such change depend on whether those who lead the change do so in response to the will of Heaven and the popular desire of the people. In modern times, the term is used as an expression meaning revolution, denoting major social, political or economic changes.

CITATION

Heaven and earth change and four seasons take place. King Tang of Shang and King Wu of Zhou changed the mandate, obeying Heaven and complying with the wishes of the people. (*The Book of Changes*)

120

géwù-zhìzhī
格物致知

Study Things to Acquire Knowledge

The term means to understand how we should conduct ourselves through our contact with things. "Studying things to acquire knowledge" comes from *The Book of Rites*. Together with "making one's purpose sincere," "correcting one's thoughts," "self-cultivation," "running one's family well," "governing the state properly," and "bringing peace to all under heaven," they are collectively known as the "eight essential principles." Knowledge is acquired through the study of things. Since the two are closely related, they are sometimes together called "study and acquire." Throughout history scholars have had varied understandings of the meaning of the term. Some emphasize a thorough inquiry of principles in contact with things. Others stress personal practice in order to master all kinds of moral conduct and skills. Still others consider their intentions as things, thus reforming their innermost thoughts as studying things.

CITATIONS

All things have their own principles. An exhaustive inquiry into the principles means the study of things. (*More Writings of the Cheng Brothers*)

Gewu (格物) means setting things right, just like what is said in *Mencius*: A great man may rectify a ruler's mind. (*Records of Great Learning*)

121

guàyáo

卦爻

Trigrams and Component Lines

A *gua* (trigram) is a system of symbols consisting of undivided lines (—) and divided lines (– –). The undivided line (—) is a yang line while the divided one (– –) a yin line. Three lines make a trigram, and there are eight such trigrams. When six lines are put together, they together make 64 hexagram combinations. Trigrams and component lines were created partly for the purpose of divination. Ancient Chinese people used yarrow stalks to make hexagrams, calculated the variations they suggested, and consulted them for the purpose of divination. Later on, people used trigrams symbolically to explain the changes and the laws regulating the changes that occurred in people and everything else, and why and how these changes took place.

CITATIONS

When the eight trigrams were invented, they embodied the images of all things. When the eight trigrams were multiplied by eight trigrams and permuted into the 64 hexagrams, all the 384 lines were included. (*The Book of Changes*)

When sages saw the changes or events happening under heaven, they observed the similarities of the events and responded with appropriate rites and rituals. They judged their implications of the changes by obtaining explanations from the *yao*. (*The Book of Changes*)

122

guójiā
国家

Family-state / Country

Family-state referred to the land owned by feudal lords and officials in ancient China. The land of a feudal lord was called "state" and the land of an official was called "family." In ancient China, family, clan and country shared common structural features, all founded on the basis of blood relationships. This is the so-called "commensurability of family and state." Family-state later referred to the entire territory of a country. In modern times, the term is also used to denote a polity encompassing a territory, a people, and a government.

CITATIONS

A man of virtue and talent should be aware of potential danger in time of peace, keep in mind possible peril in time of security, and be vigilant of turmoil in time of order. Then he can keep himself safe and his country preserved. (*The Book of Changes*)

People often say, "State and family are all under heaven." The root of all under heaven is in the state. The root of a state is in the family. (*Mencius*)

123

guótǐ

国体

Guoti

The term, literally meaning the state and the body, has three meanings. First, it refers to the important ministers who help the sovereign ruler govern the state. Figuratively, the term suggests that the state is a human body and the ministers are the major components of the body. Second, it refers to the constitution and laws of a state. Third, it means national polity or dignity.

CITATIONS

Ministers are like the arms and legs of the sovereign ruler. They constitute the major components of the country. (Fan Ning: *Annotations on Guliang's Commentary on The Spring and Autumn Annals*)

The national legal system is well enacted, and the laws and regulations are orderly implemented. (Yao Ying: A Letter to General Lu)

124

guòyóubùjí

过犹不及

Going Too Far Is as Bad as Falling Short.

It is just as bad to go beyond a given standard as to fall short of it. Confucian scholars use rites as the standards both for individuals' words and actions, and for their relationship with everything in the world. They also judge people's words or actions against the requirements of the rites to see whether they have gone too far or fallen short. Confucius evaluated one of his students as "going too far" and another as "falling short," considering them to be the same in both failing the requirements set by the rites. If a person can follow the middle way by not going too far or falling short, then he has achieved the virtue of "the Golden Mean."

CITATION

Zigong asked Confucius, "Which one is more virtuous, Zizhang or Zixia?" Confucius replied, "Zizhang tends to go too far, while Zixia often falls short." Zigong further asked, "In that case, is Zizhang better?" Confucius said, "Going too far is just as bad as falling short." (*The Analects*)

125

hǎinèi

海内

Within the Four Seas

Within the Four Seas means within the territory of China. The ancient Chinese thought China's territory was surrounded by the Four Seas (the East, West, North, and South seas). Within the Four Seas refers to the landmass surrounded by the Four Seas. It reflected the ancient Chinese belief that the seas were the natural boundary of a country, demonstrating the influence of an agriculture civilization.

CITATIONS

If our country wants to conquer all under heaven, rise above the big powers, subdue enemy states, control the territory within the Four Seas, govern the subjects and rule over the feudal lords, military force is indispensable. (*Strategies of the Warring States*)

If you have a bosom friend within the Four Seas, even at world's end he remains close to you. (Wang Bo: Seeing Off a Friend Who Has Been Appointed to a County Post in Shuzhou)

126

hǎiwài

海外

Outside the Four Seas / Overseas

Outside the Four Seas refers to the territory outside China, foreign lands, or remote areas. The ancient Chinese thought that China's territory was surrounded by the Four Seas (the East, West, North, and South seas). Therefore, places outside China were outside the Four Seas. It reflected the ancient Chinese belief that the seas were the natural boundary of a country. It also suggested that the ancient Chinese were on the one hand self-focused and on the other open-minded, longing to explore the unknown world outside the Four Seas.

CITATION

Xiangtu was so brave that he was recognized and extolled even by those outside the Four Seas. (*The Book of Songs*)

127

hé' érbùtóng

和而不同

Harmony But Not Uniformity

The term means achieving overall harmonious co-existence on the basis of respecting differences and diversity. Uniformity and harmony are two different attitudes to treating and accommodating social groups. Uniformity means obliterating differences in everything while harmony is to keep and respect the differences. Allowing different things to complement and supplement each other will create a harmonious whole full of vitality and creativity.

CITATIONS

Harmony begets new things; while uniformity does not lead to continuation. (*Discourses on Governance of the States*)

A man of virtue pursues harmony but does not seek uniformity; a petty man seeks uniformity but does not pursue harmony. (*The Analects*)

128

hòudé-zàiwù

厚德载物

Have Ample Virtue and Carry All Things

This term means that one should be broad-minded and care for all things and people. Ancient Chinese believed that with its topography and other natural features being generous and peaceful, the earth sustained all things in the world, allowing them to grow and develop in keeping with their own nature. Men of virtue model themselves on the earth, and just like the earth, care for all things and fellow human beings with open heart and virtue. This embodies the pursuit of moral cultivation and harmony among people and between people and nature. It represents the Chinese views and ideals on governance and human relationship, which were inspired by the formation and features of mountains and rivers in China. Together with the notion of constantly exerting oneself for self-improvement, it forms the fundamental character of the Chinese nation.

CITATIONS

Just like the earth, which is generous and peaceful, a man of virtue should have ample virtue and accommodate all things. (*The Book of Changes*)

The peaceful nature of the earth is due to its virtue of generosity. Thus, it can accommodate and provide for all things. By modeling himself on the earth, a man of virtue should care for all people and all things. (Chen Menglei: *A Simple Account of The Book of Changes*)

129

huà gāngē wéi yùbó
化干戈为玉帛

Beat Swords into Plowshares / Turn War into Peace

The term means to eliminate animosity in order to turn war into peace and turn conflicts into amity. *Gan* (干) and *ge* (戈) are two weapons of war which were used for defense and attack respectively. *Yu* (玉) and *bo* (帛) mean jades (such as jade tablets and jade ornaments) which were gifts exchanged between feudal lords and tribute paid to monarchs. In time, *yu* and *bo* acquired the meaning of peace and co-existence. This term reflects the Chinese people's long-standing aspiration for peace and goodwill to dissolve conflict and violence.

CITATION

Heaven has struck disaster, bringing our two sovereign lords (of the states of Qin and Jin) to face each other, not with jades and silks, but with the instruments of war. (*Zuo' s Commentary on The Spring and Autumn Annals*)

130

huàgōng, huàgōng

化工、画工

Magically Natural, Overly Crafted

The expressions are about the naturalness of literary and artistic works. The first one, "magically natural," means that a literary or artistic work is completed naturally and achieves the acme of perfection without any sign of craft. The second, "overly crafted," means that a work is meticulously crafted, but it is overly elaborate in style while lacking naturalness and spontaneity. "Magically natural" is used to refer to works accomplished by artists while "overly crafted" is used to describe works done by craftsmen. These two standards were proposed by Ming writer Li Zhi in his "Random Thoughts," which echoed his idea that writings must reflect the author's true sentiments. Culturally, the distinction between "magically natural" and "overly crafted" is rooted in the Daoist thought of being harmonious with nature while forsaking excessive skills. Most Ming scholars favored literary naturalism and rejected elaboration and imitation.

CITATIONS

Wu Daozi had superb technical skills, but his paintings were over crafted. What is remarkable about Wang Wei is that he gave free rein to his imagination in his paintings, like a bird that had broken free from its cage. Both of them were highly skilled, but I like Wang Wei better; I can find no fault in his works. (Su Shi: The Paintings of Wang Wei and Wu Daozi)

The Pavilion of Moon Worship and *Romance of the West Chamber* were works of magical naturalness, whereas *The Story of the Lute* was an overly crafted work. The latter shows that an attempt made to outdo the magic of nature has proved impossible to achieve. (Li Zhi: Random Thoughts)

131

huàdào

画道

Dao of Painting

The term has both broad and narrow meanings. Interpreted narrowly, it means various painting techniques. Interpreted broadly, it means the cultural values, personality, artistic style, and aesthetic aspiration embodied in a painting, suggesting a perfect fusion of Dao and skills. Dao determines the theme a painting conveys as well as the painting's artistic principles and aesthetic style. A painting is a concrete image that illustrates Dao. It reflects the cultural principles followed by the painter as well as his personality, artistic style, and aesthetic aspiration. Therefore, paintings illuminate Dao, which in turn enhances the paintings. Prominent painters seek to access Dao through refining their skills and epitomizing Dao in artwork. The Dao of painting not only encompasses the Dao of nature, but also the Dao of social life, demonstrating the commitment to humanism inherent in the Chinese culture.

CITATIONS

Sages follow Dao intellectually, while virtuous talent can access Dao. Natural scenery manifests Dao in its natural forms and shapes, cultivating a love for it in the benevolent. Isn't that wonderful? (Zong Bing: On the Creation of Landscape Painting)

The Dao of painting enables one to use his hand to depict the wonder of nature and present to viewers a scene full of life. (Dong Qichang: *Essays from Huachan Studio*)

132

huàlóng-diǎnjīng
画龙点睛

Adding Pupils to the Eyes of a Painted Dragon / Rendering the Final Touch

The term is a metaphor about giving the finishing touch, which means providing critical details or key words in an artistic or literary work in order to lend it charm and aesthetic conception. Mencius believed that when observing a person, one should look directly into his eyes because the eyes reveal his nature, be it good or evil. When painting portraits, Gu Kaizhi in the Eastern Jin Dynasty did not add pupils to the eyes in haste. He stressed that the key to painting a vivid portrait lied in painting the eyes. Zhang Sengyao, a painter of the Southern Dynasties, was well known for his excellent painting skills. Legend has it that his painted dragons flew into the sky as soon as he finished their pupils. The term is thus used by later generations to underline the importance of applying critical touches to add life and charm to a literary or artistic work.

CITATION

Zhang Sengyao painted four white dragons on the wall of the Anle Temple in Nanjing. But he did not paint pupils to their eyes, saying that once he did, the dragons would fly into the sky. People considered his words absurd and repeatedly urged him to add pupils to the dragons' eyes. He eventually did it on two of the four dragons. Suddenly, lightning and thunders struck, and the two dragons with pupils added to their eyes flew into the clouds. The other two remained on the wall. (Zhang Yanyuan: *Notes on Past Famous Paintings*)

133

huìxīn

会心

Heart-to-heart Communication

The term refers to a situation in which people understand each other without the need to utter a single word. It generally means the spontaneous understanding reached by close friends who share common interests, aspirations, and dispositions. In particular, it refers to an aesthetic state in which the subject and the object interact with each other smoothly with no barrier between them, or in which an artist creates a marvelous image and a viewer appreciates it with emotion and understanding. The culmination of such an experience is joy and satisfaction derived from the perfect harmony between the human heart and its surroundings.

CITATIONS

When Emperor Jianwen of Liang in the Southern Dynasties was touring the Hualin Garden, he turned to his followers and said, "A place which prompts heart-to-heart communication need not be far. This garden is shadowed by trees and has a stream meandering through. Such a place makes one think of Zhuangzi strolling on the bridge of the Haoshui River and angling in the Pushui River, where birds and fish seemed eager to get close to him." (Liu Yiqing: *A New Account of Tales of the World*)

The Book of Songs contains odes, satires, and admonitions, but all are veiled. One must engage in a heart-to-heart communication to appreciate them. (Jiang Kui: *The Poetry Theory of Baishi Daoren*)

134

hùndùn

浑沌

Chaos

The term has two meanings. First, it refers to the state of one whole mass that existed before the universe took shape, often said to exist before *qi* (vital force) emerged. The multitude of organisms on earth all emanated from this state. Second, it refers to Chaos, king of the Central Region in a fable in *Zhuangzi*. According to the fable, Chaos had no eyes, nose, mouth or ears. Shu, king of the South Sea, and Hu, king of the North Sea, drilled seven apertures into Chaos and killed him. Zhuangzi used this story to show the state of chaos of the world in which there is neither knowledge or wisdom, nor distinction between good and evil.

CITATIONS

Those who commented on *The Book of Changes* said, "Before *qi* (vital force) appeared, the world was in a state of formless chaos." (Wang Chong: *A Comparative Study of Different Schools of Learning*)

The king of the South Sea was called Shu, the king of the North Sea was called Hu, and the king of the Central Region was called Chaos. Shu and Hu often met in the territory of Chaos, who treated them very well. They wanted to repay his kindness, and said, "Every man has seven apertures with which to hear, to see, to eat and drink, and to breathe, but Chaos alone has none of them. Let's try and bore some for him." They bored one aperture on Chaos each day, and on the seventh day Chaos died. (*Zhuangzi*)

135

huófǎ

活法

Literary Flexibility

Literary flexibility means that one should respect the rules for writing poetry or prose but not be bound by them; one should encourage change and innovation. The opposite of literary flexibility is literary rigidity under whose influence the writer mechanically imitates the forms of established writers without innovation. One way to attain literary flexibility in one's works is to draw inspiration from others extensively and absorb their talent while refraining from sticking mechanically to the model. One should base oneself on his own feelings and the aesthetic principles so as to create new styles and new ways of expression. Influenced by the Chan spirit of liberal flexibility, literary critics of the Song Dynasty championed flexibility in literary pursuit and established it as an important principle guiding poetry and prose writing.

CITATIONS

Those who wish to learn to write poetry should master literary flexibility. By this I mean that, while knowing all the rules for poetry, the poet goes beyond them to reflect unpredictable changes in his poetry yet without compromising the rules. The principle underlying this way of writing is that there should be set rules, yet they are not fixed; where there seem to be no rules, rules do exist. You can discuss literary flexibility with others only if they understand this principle. (Lü Benzhong: Foreword to *The Collected Poetry of Xia Junfu*)

In writing essays, it is necessary to maintain literary flexibility. If one is bound by the clichés of the classical masters and fails to produce novel ideas, this is what we call literary rigidity. Literary rigidity refers to mechanically copying others without permitting one's own work to acquire new ideas. Literary flexibility, however, allows one's work to free itself from clichés so that the work will not be stifled by stereotyped style of writing. Literary rigidity leads to a literary dead end, while literary flexibility encourages the birth of new ideas by going beyond the limitations of conventional way of writing. (Yu Cheng: *Reflections from Devoted Reading*)

136

jiān'ài

兼爱

Universal Love

Universal love, equal affection for all individuals, is a basic concept of the Mohist School of thought, as opposed to the principle of differentiated love advocated by the Confucian School. Universal love emphasizes that you should love others as you love yourself, and love others' relatives and people of other states as you love your own so that all people would love one another equally. This principle of affection has no regard for blood ties or social status. It is an affection that is exercised equally without differentiating between individuals, families, or nations. If such a principle could be realized, we could avoid conflicts between persons, clans, or nations and bring equal benefit to all.

CITATION

Universal love will bring peace and order to the world while mutual animosity can only throw the world into disorder. (*Mozi*)

137

jiěyī-pánbó
解衣盘礴

Sitting with Clothes Unbuttoned and Legs Stretching Out

The term originally referred to the appearance of an artist who is concentrating on painting. It has been extended to mean an unrestrained state of mind free from external interruption when an artist is doing creative work. The book *Zhuangzi* describes a painter drawing freely with his clothes thrown open and legs stretching out. "To unbutton one's clothes" is to expose one's chest and arms; and "to sit with legs stretching out" indicates a casual posture while one is concentrating on painting. This term stresses the importance of a relaxed state and complete freedom of mind to the successful creation of quality artwork. This concept had significant influence on subsequent development of theories on calligraphy and painting in later generations.

CITATIONS

Once when King Yuan of the State of Song was to do painting, all the painters came. Half of them, after paying him their respects, stood submissively to prepare brush-pen and ink for him. The other half were waiting outside. One painter, however, arrived late and was casual in manner. After receiving the king's instructions, he returned to his hostel instead of standing there respectfully. The king sent somebody to check on him, and he was seen sitting there painting attentively with his chest and shoulders exposed and both legs stretching out. The king exclaimed, "Yes, that is a real painter!" (*Zhuangzi*)

When doing painting, one should unbutton one's clothes, sit with legs stretching out, keep himself free from all external interruptions, and ignore spectators. That way, one is able to obtain miraculous creative power, draw inspirations from heaven, earth, and nature, go beyond the rules of previous painting masters, and freely use various painting techniques. (Yun Shouping: *Nantian's Comments on Paintings*)

138

jing (jīngshī)
京（京师）

Capital of a Country

This term refers to the place where the Son of Heaven resided and conducted state affairs. *Jing* (京) originally meant a big hill or mound, representing the idea of being big or grand, and *shi* (师) meant a lot of people. To name the place where the Son of Heaven resided and conducted state affairs *jing* or *jingshi* (京师) suggests that the capital is huge in size and expresses reverence towards the Son of Heaven.

CITATION

What does *jingshi* mean? It is the place where the Son of Heaven resides. What does *jing* mean? It means grandeur and magnificence. What does *shi* mean? It means a lot of people. No words other than populous and grandeur can best describe the place where the Son of Heaven lives. (*Gongyang's Commentary on The Spring and Autumn Annals*)

139

jīngjì
经济

To Govern and Help the People

The term is an abbreviation of an expression meaning public governance and support for the people. *Jing* (经) means managing state and social affairs in an orderly manner; *ji* (济) means helping people who are in difficulty. This dual-pronged approach to governance is aimed at making the nation and society prosperous and ensuring that the people live in peace and contentment. The concept of *jingji* (经济) embodies the goals and principles followed by traditional Chinese intellectuals in the pursuit of scholarship and learning, and reflects their commitment to apply learning to the service of the country and for the benefit of the people. In modern times, the term is used to mean "economy," namely, social activities that create, transfer or realize value, and satisfy people's material and cultural needs.

CITATIONS

The state selects talent through imperial civil service examinations solely on the basis of their literary ability and qualifies scholars only on the basis of their knowledge of the classics. This is ignoring the truly important and choosing the trivial. Even if we have an abundance of candidates, it will be hard to pick one or two competent ones out of every ten. In the current dire situation facing the empire and with paucity of talent, how can we save the country? Only by teaching scholars how to govern and help the people and by selecting talent in those areas can we hope to meet the demand for competent professionals. (Fan Zhongyan: Presentation of Ten Proposals in Response to Emperor Renzong's Proclamation)

Why is it that there have been so few people adept at governance and helping the people since ancient times? (Du Fu: Reflections While Going Upstream)

140

jīngshì-zhìyòng
经世致用

Study of Ancient Classics Should Meet Present Needs.

Learning should contribute to good governance. *Jingshi* (经世) means governance of the country and society, and *zhiyong* (致用) refers to meeting practical needs. In the early 17th century, thinkers such as Gu Yanwu, Wang Fuzhi, Huang Zongxi, and Li Yong argued that scholarly studies should be geared to meet current needs. They held that while interpreting ancient classics, scholars should expound their views on the social and political issues of their day, solve practical problems, enhance governance of the country, improve people's livelihood, and promote social reform. This view stressed the practical value of knowledge and the practical responsibilities of intellectuals. It reflects the pragmatic character of traditional Chinese intellectuals as well as their concern for the well-being of the people and eagerness to shoulder responsibility for the whole nation.

CITATIONS

No articles should be written except those that are concerned with what the Six Classics teach us about the current state affairs. (Gu Yanwu: Letters to a Friend)

Scholars should value knowledge of current affairs. Memorials to the throne should be about such affairs... There should be no empty talk on abstract theories. The value of knowledge lies in dealing with practical matters. Scholars whose studies do not reveal the essence of things or put forward ways of coping with difficult situations should feel ashamed as an uneducated woman! (Li Yong: *Collected Works of Li Yong*)

My late father was very diligent. He read a wide range of works, from Neo-Confucian theories to books on dealing with practical matters. There was nothing he did not study in depth. (Cui Shu: An Account of My Late Father)

141

jìngjiè
境界

Jingjie (Visionary World)

Jingjie (境界) originally meant border or boundary. Later, it was used to translate the idea of a mental realm in Buddhist sutras, a state of spiritual cultivation achieved after having overcome bewilderment in the material world. As a literary and artistic term, *jingjie* is mainly used to indicate the aesthetic depth in a literary work so as to give full expression to the author's creativity, comprehension, and aesthetic faculties. A work reaching a high level of *jingjie* manifests the author's true personality, transcends the ordinary, strikes a responsive chord in the heart of the reader, stimulates the reader's imagination, and thus enhances the reader's appreciation of his work. The term *yijing* (意境 aesthetic conception) came into being earlier than *jingjie*, which was formed under the influence of Buddhism in the mid-Tang period. In his *Poetic Remarks in the Human World*, modern scholar Wang Guowei wrote extensively about *jingjie*. He often used *yijing* in the same sense as he used *jingjie* or the other way round. He created the theory of *jingjie*, in which he blended classical Western and classical Chinese aesthetics. Generally speaking, *yijing* refers to a perfect combination of the message the author conveys with the images he uses in his works, and it gives full rein to reader's imagination. The concept of *jingjie*, however, foregrounds the sublimation of artistic images through mental insight, and emphasizes the role of the mental world in elevating the work of art to a higher level.

CITATIONS

The visionary world achieved in literary works serves as a better criterion for making critical evaluation than one's personal character or charm. The visionary world is primary, whereas one's personal character and charm are secondary. Once the visionary world is reached, personal character and charm will naturally follow. (Wang Guowei: *Poetic Remarks in the Human World [Reduced Version]*)

Painting landscapes is about depicting with brush and ink the artist's affective response to a natural scene. When the artist's sentiments interact intensely with the natural scene, a realm of what we call the visionary world is reached. (Buyantu: How to Paint)

142

jìng shēng xiàng wài

境生象外

Aesthetic Conception Transcends Concrete Objects Described.

The aesthetic conception evoked by a poem or prose transcends what a physical object denotes, and a reader needs to perceive and appreciate the beauty of such aesthetic conception. *Jing* (境) here refers to an aesthetic conception created by a poem or prose, while *xiang* (象) refers to the image of a concrete object portrayed in such writing. Composed of words, a poem describes individual objects through which it evokes a coherent poetic conception beyond the physical appearance of such objects. This proposition was first put forward by poet Liu Yuxi of the Tang Dynasty to express his understanding of poetry. He pointed out that words and images were concrete while aesthetic conceptions were abstract and subtle and therefore hard to describe. Liu's proposition, namely, aesthetic conception transcending concrete objects described, marked an important stage in the development of the theory of aesthetic conception in classical Chinese poetry.

CITATIONS

Aesthetic conception and imagery are not the same thing, and it is not always easy to distinguish between what is actual and what is implied. Some things like scenery can be seen but not taken, while others such as wind can be heard but not seen. Still others are like thought: it exists in our body but is not restricted by the body. Some pervades everything but possesses no particular shape, like color. All these can be expressed concretely or indirectly by implication. (Jiaoran: *Comments on Poetry*)

Is poetry highly condensed prose? A poem can convey the same meaning of a prose without using many words. Therefore, poetry is implicit and subtle, an art that is hard to master. Poetic conception often transcends what is denoted by the objects described, therefore it is subtle and difficult to achieve. (Liu Yuxi: Preface to *Dong's Wu Ling Ji*)

143

jū'ān-sīwēi

居安思危

Be on Alert Against Potential Danger When Living in Peace

One should always be on alert against potential danger in time of peace. All ambitious rulers in history hoped to maintain enduring stability. They often reminded themselves not to indulge in pleasure and comfort, but to conduct diligent governance, work hard to make their country prosperous, and resolve social conflicts in a timely manner so as to prevent them from developing into crises. This keen awareness of potential danger was a quality of accomplished rulers in Chinese history. This notion has also become a principle for modern enterprise management, and been adopted by common people in their pursuit of progress.

CITATION

If one keeps thinking about danger that could emerge, then there can be safety; if one keeps reminding oneself of the possible outbreak of war, then there can be peace; if one keeps thinking about the possible fall of the nation, then the nation can be preserved. (Wu Jing: *Important Political Affairs of the Zhenguan Reign*)

144

jūn

君

Lord / Nobility / Monarch

Originally, the term referred to the Son of Heaven, dukes or princes, ministers, and senior officials who owned land and ruled the common people. It later referred to ducal monarchs and the emperor only. The Chinese character 君 is composed of two parts, namely, 尹 and 口. The top part 尹 means to run a country and govern its people, and the lower part 口 means to give orders. Ancient Chinese believed that a monarch or nobility must possess four qualities: first, having extraordinary virtues and be competent; second, having the mandate of Heaven; third, in possession of land or manor; and fourth, having the ability to govern officials and common people, and enjoying their unfailing loyalty.

CITATIONS

The Son of Heaven, dukes or princes, ministers, and senior officials who own land are all regarded as the nobility or lord. (Zheng Xuan: *Annotations on The Book of Rites and Rituals*)

The lord, monarch or nobility rules over common people who pledge loyalty to their authority. (*Debates of the White Tiger Hall*)

145

jūnzǐ

君子

Junzi (Man of Virtue)

Junzi (君子) was originally used to indicate a person's social status, generally referring to a ruler or a member of the aristocracy. Beginning with Confucius, the term acquired an additional moral dimension and came to mean someone of true virtue. The opposite of *junzi* is *xiaoren* (小人), which roughly means the "petty men." In the Confucian tradition, *junzi* is someone who is above a scholar and below a sage in terms of moral influence. A man of virtue pursues and practices the ideal known as Dao and regards Dao as the fundamental meaning of life above power or gains.

CITATIONS

A man of virtue understands and observes what is morally right; while a petty man only has his eyes on and goes after what brings personal gains. (*The Analects*)

A man of virtue is someone who has achieved moral integrity. (Zhu Xi: *The Analects Variorum*)

146

kāiwù-chéngwù

开物成务

Understand Things and Succeed in One's Endeavors

This term means to find out the truth of things, and act accordingly to succeed in what one does. *Kaiwu* (开物) means to reveal the truth of things and understand their intrinsic relations and rules. *Chengwu* (成务) means to use proper methods to do things successfully according to their intrinsic relations and rules. This was a perception and guide to action that the ancient Chinese learned from *The Book of Changes* and everyday life, which they used to understand the world, change the world, and serve themselves. This concept represents a fundamental principle of social science.

CITATION

The Book of Changes aims to reveal the truth of all things on earth, point out how to handle affairs, and do them right. It covers the basic rules governing all things on earth. *(The Book of Changes)*

147

kūn
坤

Kun

One of the eight trigrams, *kun* (坤) consists of three yin lines: ☷. It is also one of the 64 hexagrams when it consists of six yin lines: ䷁. According to scholars on *The Book of Changes,* as the *kun* trigram is composed only of yin lines, it is purely yin and is thus used to symbolize all yin things or principles. The *kun* trigram symbolizes earth, and when it comes to society, it symbolizes the social roles played the by the female, the mother, and the subjects of the ruler, as well as gentle, kind, and generous ways of doing things. In this context, *kun* also means creating and nourishing all things under heaven.

CITATIONS

The *kun* trigram means gentleness. (*The Book of Changes*)

Great is the *kun* hexagram! All things owe their existence to *kun,* since it represents the will of Heaven. (*The Book of Changes*)

148

lǐ
礼

Li (Rites / Social Norms)

Li (礼) is a general term for social norms which regulate an individual's relationship with other people, everything else in nature, and even ghosts and spirits. By setting various regulations about ceremonial vessels, rituals, and systems, rites define an individual's specific status and corresponding duty and power, thereby differentiating between people in a community in terms of age, kinship, and social status. With such differentiations, the rites determine the proper position of each individual, thus achieving harmony among human beings, and between humanity and everything else in nature.

CITATIONS

Rites are the rules governing the movement of heaven and earth as well as code of conduct for the people. (*Zuo's Commentary on The Spring and Autumn Annals*)

Rites are the basis for determining proper human relations, clarifying ambiguities, differentiating between things, and telling right from wrong. (*The Book of Rites*)

Rites are observed to achieve harmony. Former kings followed this principle in handling matters both great and small, and were praised for doing so. But sometimes acting in such a way alone is not adequate. If one pursues harmony simply because it is so precious as to forgo the constraints of rites, the result will not be desirable. (*The Analects*)

149

miàowù

妙悟

Subtle Insight

This term refers to an inner experience one gains under special circumstances. When the mind is so relaxed and peaceful, it allows one to develop an intimate appreciation and understanding of beauty and then express it in a poem. The beauty of the poem thus inspired transcends words and creates an intense aesthetic experience. Subtle insight enables the reader to appreciate the essence and lasting beauty of a poem by creating a spontaneous experience so engrossing that one becomes oblivious to both himself and the outside world. According to Buddhist, Daoist, and Metaphysical principles, "subtle" refers to the minute and profound nature of thinking, whereas "insight" is an intensely personal experience derived not from logical reasoning. Chan Buddhism promotes meditation as a way to return to the mind's original tranquility and thus achieve a clear and simple state of mind. Such a state of mind comes from literary and artistic experience. In *Canglang's Criticism of Poetry*, literary critic Yan Yu of the Southern Song Dynasty dealt extensively with the function and features of subtle insight in poetry writing by drawing on Chan philosophy. This book is the first one to apply Chan terms to critical writing on poetry and has thus gained great influence. The concept of subtle insight has also influenced traditional painting and calligraphy in China.

CITATIONS

By concentrating one's mind and freeing one's thoughts, one can reach such a fascinating state in appreciating the beauty of nature as to become oblivious to the outside world and one's own self, totally free from the constraints of physical forms and limitations of knowledge. (Zhang Yanyuan: *Notes on Past Famous Paintings*)

Generally speaking, the most important principle of meditation is to achieve subtle insight, and this is the most important principle underlying poetry writing as well. For example, while Meng Haoran is no equal to Han Yu in terms of knowledge and talent, his poems surpass those of Han Yu because he is able to create subtle insight. (Yan Yu: *Canglang's Criticism of Poetry*)

150

mínbāo-wùyǔ

民胞物与

All People Are My Brothers and Sisters, and All Things Are My Companions.

This idea was first put forward by Zhang Zai of the Northern Song Dynasty, who held that people and things are all created by the vital force of heaven and earth, and thus are similar in nature. He advocated love for all people and things in the world, and his view transcended the old anthropocentric viewpoint and aimed to reach harmony between oneself and other human beings as well as between oneself and other creatures and things. It is the same as the idea that a true gentleman has ample virtue and cares for all things. This notion is an important part of the School of Principle of the Song and Ming dynasties.

CITATION

Therefore, what fills heaven and earth constitutes my body; what governs heaven and earth forms my nature. All people are my brothers and sisters, and all things are my companions. (Zhang Zai: *The Western Inscription*)

151

míngshí

名实

Name and Substance

Shi (实) refers to an existing object, while *ming* (名) refers to a name, a title or an appellation given to an object. A name is given on the basis of substance, and it cannot be separated from the knowledge of the substance. Names give expression to people's understanding about the essence of objects and their interrelations, and the way in which they handle such interrelations. By giving names, people integrate all things and all objects into a certain order. The position and significance of an object in the whole system are determined on the basis of the name, title or the appellation given to it.

CITATIONS

That by which an object is called is the name. That which a name refers to is a substance. (*Mozi*)

An object has a shape, and a shape has a name. The name must not go beyond the substance, and the substance must not extend beyond its name. (*Guanzi*)

152

mìng

命

Mandate / Destiny

The earliest meaning of the term was mandate of Heaven, that is, the intentions and instructions that Heaven expressed to humans. The implication was that Heaven meted out rewards and punishments on human beings as their moral conduct deserved. The mandate of Heaven was considered an irresistible force that determined dynastic changes, the rise and fall of nations, and even the fate of ordinary people. Later, the link with Heaven became weaker; instead, the unavoidable destiny or fate prevailed. For human beings, the term implies the external limits that determine what is possible and what is not. In one sense, it expresses the helplessness of human beings.

CITATIONS

The mandate of Heaven is not immutable. (*The Book of Songs*)

Knowing that one cannot change his destiny, one should face things calmly and submit himself to fate. (*Zhuangzi*)

153

qìxiàng
气象

Prevailing Features

Qixiang (气象), originally a term about the general state of scenery and physical objects in nature, also refers to the prevailing features of a society in a given period of time. This description carries the meaning of great appeal and impact as well as scenery and objects. When applied to art, it refers to the overall style and appeal in a piece of artistic work. It connotes grandeur and magnificence, and is often used in conjunction with such words as "heroic," "immense," and "sublime." Literary critics of the Tang Dynasty began using the term to comment on the style and features of a poem or an essay. Since the Song Dynasty, the term has become an important concept in literary criticism, used to critique the style and artistic flair of poems, essays, calligraphy, and paintings. It is often thought to reflect the prevailing features in literature and art of a particular period. For instance, during the prime of the Tang Dynasty, the term referred to the appeal of both poems and the poets who wrote them.

CITATIONS

Works of many poets during the prime of the Tang Dynasty struck readers with their powerful expression, just like the calligraphy of Yan Zhenqing. (Yan Yu: Letter in Reply to Uncle Wu Jingxian in Lin'an)

Generally speaking, one should strive to achieve an elegant style and powerful expression in writing. However, as a writer becomes more experienced, his writing will grow simple and natural in style. (Zhou Zizhi: *Zhupo's Poetry Comments*)

Regarding five-character-a-line verses, only Du Fu's poems possess a style that is imposing and original and a quality that is both profound and forceful. (Hu Yinglinf: *An In-depth Exploration of Poetry*)

154

qián

乾

Qian

One of the eight trigrams, it consists of three yang lines: ☰. It is also one of the 64 hexagrams when it consists of six yang lines: ䷀. According to scholars on *The Book of Changes*, as the *qian* trigram is composed only of yang lines, it is purely yang and is thus used to symbolize all yang things or principles. The *qian* trigram symbolizes heaven, and in social terms, it symbolizes the social roles played by the male, the father, and the monarch, as well as decisive and vigorous ways of doing things. In this context, *qian* also means creating and leading all things under heaven.

CITATIONS

The *qian* trigram symbolizes vigor and vitality. (*The Book of Changes*)

Great is the *qian* hexagram! All things owe their existence to it, and it guides the movement of heaven and creates its impact. (*The Book of Changes*)

155

qǔjìng
取境

Qujing (Conceptualize an Aestheric Feeling)

The term means to conceptualize an aesthetic feeling by selecting images that best express a poet's sentiments and appreciation. The term *qujing* (取境) was coined by the Tang monk poet Jiaoran in his *Poetic Styles*. After conducting a review of how poets from the Six Dynasties to the mid-Tang Dynasty wrote poems, he concluded that to write poems, one must structure one's thoughts ingeniously so as to generate a uniquely original conception with no trace of clichés. Then, after some deep thinking, an inspiration will arise and his imagination will run free. In this way, the poet can create a poem with a fine visionary world. Although the conception may be highly original, ultimately the style of the work should be simple and natural without any traces of having been laboriously crafted. This term is closely related to the terms *jingjie* (境界) and *yijing* (意境); together, they are part of a series of terms dealing with *jing* (境) in classical Chinese poetics.

CITATIONS

When a poet starts to compose a poem, if his conception of the poem tends towards grandeur, then the artistic conception of the poem will be grand; if his conception of the poem is free and easy, so will be the aesthetic conception of the poem. (Jiaoran: *Poetic Styles*)

Without entering the tiger's den, one cannot catch a cub. When developing one's poetic conception, it is necessary to begin to contemplate what is most difficult and daring before great lines can spring to mind. After one completes a poem, one should review its overall structure and appeal. If it looks so smooth and natural as if written effortlessly, then it will be a great poem. (Jiaoran: *Poetic Styles*)

156

réndào

人道

Way of Man

The way of man refers to the code of conduct that people must observe and also the relations and norms that keep human society on the right track. The way of man stands in contrast to the way of heaven. When Western culture was introduced to China in modern times, the term gained the meaning of respect and care for people's lives, well-being, dignity, freedom, and individuality.

CITATIONS

The way of heaven is far away; the way of man is near. (*Zuo's Commentary on The Spring and Autumn Annals*)

The rise of Yao and Shun did not change the sun and the moon. The fall of Jie and Zhou did not change the stars. This is because the way of man does not change the way of heaven. (Lu Jia: *New Thoughts*)

157

rénwén

人文

Renwen

Renwen (人文) encompasses the cultural and ethical progress created by rites, music, education, codes, and systems as well as a social order which is hierarchical but harmonious. *Renwen* is in contrast to *tianwen* (天文), the study of celestial bodies including the sun, moon, and stars. *Renwen* also refers to human affairs in general, that is, behaviors, customs, and the human state. Under the influence of Western culture in the modern period, *renwen* came to mean cultural phenomena in human society as well as the humanities, which are academic disciplines that study human culture.

CITATIONS

By observing heavenly patterns, we can learn about the change of times; by observing human cultural patterns, we can educate the people and build a thriving, prosperous, and refined society. (*The Book of Changes*)

When the movement of celestial bodies is manifest, we can infer from it changes of the times, which is about the distribution and movement of celestial bodies as well as climate change. When sages disseminate their vision in writing to educate the people and build a thriving, prosperous, and refined society, that is about human culture. To learn about the actual changes of the visible and the invisible and the subtle relations between heaven and humans, it is essential to study both natural phenomena and human culture. (*The History of the Northern Qi Dynasty*)

158

sānxuán

三玄

Three Metaphysical Classics

The term refers to three metaphysical works: *Laozi, Zhuangzi,* and *The Book of Changes*. During the Han Dynasty, the study of the Five Classics was the prevailing trend; but during the Wei and Jin dynasties, the way of thinking changed considerably. Scholars turned their attention to *Laozi, Zhuangzi,* and *The Book of Changes*. The annotations by such people as He Yan, Wang Bi, Xiang Xiu, and Guo Xiang gave these classics new meanings. The Three Metaphysical Classics were the focus of discourse among leading scholars of the Wei and Jin dynasties, and they were regarded by scholars of metaphysic learning as a source of inspiration when they expressed their philosophical thinking. The study of the Three Metaphysical Classics focused on probing the contradiction between individual life and the outside world. It also fully demonstrated conflict and complementarity between the thinking of Confucian and Daoist scholars.

CITATION

In the Liang Dynasty, there was a renewed interest in the study of *Zhuangzi, Laozi,* and *The Book of Changes*, which were collectively referred to as the Three Metaphysical Classics. (Yan Zhitui: *Admonitions for the Yan Clan*)

159

shàngdì

上帝

Supreme Ruler / Ruler of Heaven

The term has two meanings. One is the supreme ruler of the universe, also known as the Ruler of Heaven. During the Shang and Zhou dynasties, wizards were the intermediaries between humans and the supreme ruler. They asked for his orders by means of divination and conveyed them to humans. The other meaning is the supreme ruler of an empire or dynasty, that is, the emperor or monarch, including those of remote antiquity and those who had died; each was referred to as Son of Heaven. After Christianity was introduced to China, missionaries used this term as a translation of the word "God."

CITATIONS

Former kings thus created music to extol virtue, conducted grand ceremonies to honor the Ruler of Heaven, and worshipped ancestral tablets. (*The Book of Changes*)

August is the Ruler of Heaven, beholding the mortal world in majesty. He surveys and watches the four quarters, bringing peace and stability to the people. (*The Book of Songs*)

160

shàngshànruòshuǐ

上善若水

Great Virtue Is Like Water.

The greatest virtue is just like water, nurturing all things without competing with them. This term was first used by Laozi to advocate the belief that a virtuous ruler should govern with gentle and accommodating qualities as demonstrated by water. He should assist and provide for people just like what the water does, instead of competing with them for resources. Later, this term came to mean that people should nourish all things as water does and try their best to help people without seeking fame or profit. It also refers to human virtues such as endurance for the sake of achieving a noble goal and modesty.

CITATION

Great virtue is like water. Water nourishes all things gently and does not compete with anything, content to be in a low place not sought by people. Water is therefore closest to Dao. (*Laozi*)

161

shén yǔ wù yóu

神与物游

Interaction Between the Mind and the Subject Matter

This term refers to the creative process through which a writer interacts with subject matter and gives free rein to his imagination. During the process, he projects onto real objects his mental sensations and imaginings, and endows them with an aesthetic tone. Conversely, his imaginary sensations and imaginings are given concrete expression by real objects. The free interaction between mind and subject matter, transcending the limitations of space and time, creates a superb artistic work depicted in language. The term originated in the words of "taking advantage of the circumstances to let your mind wander freely" in *Zhuangzi*. Later, this idea was systematically developed by Liu Xie in *The Literary Mind and the Carving of Dragons* during the Southern Dynasties to describe imaginative contemplation. The term stresses the importance of interaction between the mind and the poetic subject matter as well as free imagination in the process of artistic creation. It demonstrates the process of thinking in artistic creation and succinctly summarizes the underlying features of aesthetic appreciation and freedom in artistic creation.

CITATIONS

When starting to write an essay, one should keep away sounds and sights and keep his mind focused so as to allow the imagination to search freely in the universe. When his mind reaches the farthest end, all confusion will dissipate, and images will clearly emerge in his mind one after another. (Lu Ji: *The Art of Writing*)

What is marvelous about composing a poem is that it makes it possible for the mind and the imagination to interact freely with external objects. The feelings and imaginings that well up from within are determined by a writer's aspirations and temperament. We recognize external objects through hearing and vision, but these objects are expressed through the use of language. (Liu Xie: *The Literary Mind and the Carving of Dragons*)

162

shényùn

神韵

Elegant Subtlety

This term refers to the subtle elegance of literary and artistic works. It was originally used to depict a person's mien and manner. During the Wei and Jin dynasties, the propriety inherent in a person was valued, whereas during the previous Han Dynasty, a person's external appearance was stressed. Later on, this concept was incorporated into the theory of calligraphy and painting to refer to the elegant subtlety of a work. In the Ming Dynasty, the concept was extended to the theory of poetry, and elegant subtlety became a requirement for composing poetry. Later, Wang Shizhen of the Qing Dynasty further developed the theory of elegant subtlety. In compiling *The Elegant Subtlety of the Tang Poetry*, he elaborated on his aesthetic views. In his writings on poetry theory, Wang Shizhen championed these views and created his own unique poetical aesthetics, enriching the theory of elegant subtlety, and making it a major school of the Qing-dynasty poetics.

CITATIONS

Just as gentle breeze touching one's face and the river flowing past, a good poem has elegant subtlety permeating its lines. (Lu Shiyong: *A Comprehensive Digest of Good Ancient Poems*)

I have read the works by poets of the late Tang Dynasty and the Five Dynasties and found their poetry mean-spirited, trivial, and depressed. They were far less bold and daring than those poems written between the Kaiyuan and Yuanhe periods of the Tang Dynasty. Worse still, they did not have the slightest traces of the elegant subtlety and inspiring imagery that were evident in the poetry written in the State of Chen during the Northern Dynasties and in the Sui Dynasty when poetry was already in decline. (Wang Shizhen: Foreword to *Poetry by the Mei Family*)

163

shīchū-yǒumíng
师出有名

Fighting a War with a Moral Justification

To wage a war, one must have a legitimate cause, just as we ought to have such a reason in doing all things. The term has two meanings. The first is that moral justification is a source of strength when waging a war. With moral justification, the troops will have high morale and strength in fighting. Without it, it would be difficult to command the troops. The second meaning is that war must not be waged without a just cause. Greed or anger should not be allowed to lead to militarism and aggression. The underlying notion of this concept is that war can only be fought with a just cause, which represents the spirit of civilization.

CITATIONS

A military campaign must have a moral justification. (*The Book of Rites*)

Those who have virtue thrive; those who go against virtue perish. If a war is waged without moral justification, it will not succeed. (*The History of the Han Dynasty*)

I hope the voice of justice will be heard everywhere. Be bold and confident when fighting a just war. When a military campaign has a moral justification, great victory can be achieved. (Zhu Ding: *A Tale of a Jade Dressing Table*)

164

shīshǐ

诗史

Historical Poetry

This term refers to poetry that reflects social realities and major events of a historical period, thus possessing historical value. Some of the poems in *The Book of Songs* were about the realities of its time, which prompted Confucius to exclaim that "*The Book of Songs* enables one to understand society." This means that he viewed *The Book of Songs* as using poetry to reflect history. Han-dynasty scholars stressed the importance of poetry as a means of recording history. Subsequently, Chinese scholars of poetry believed that poetry should reflect reality through aesthetic means so as to provide aesthetic enjoyment, understanding as well as education. The poems of Tang poet Du Fu are called "historical poetry" because they reflected what the country went through during the An Lushan-Shi Siming Rebellion and the author's acute sense of sadness about the misery the country and its people suffered in times of national crisis.

CITATIONS

Du Fu fled to the provinces of Gansu and Sichuan to escape turbulences caused by the An Lushan-Shi Siming Rebellion and wrote about his experiences in poems. As his poems gave vivid and detailed accounts about events of the time, they became known as "historical poetry." (Meng Qi: *The Story of Poetry*)

People regarded the poems of Du Fu as historical poetry mostly because they described what really happened in his age, and they contained criticisms or praises of historical events. So his poems were aptly called "historical poetry." (Wen Tianxiang: Preface to *The Selected Poems of Du Fu*)

165

shī zhōng yǒu huà, huà zhōng yǒu shī
诗中有画，画中有诗

Painting in Poetry, Poetry in Painting

This expression highlights the connection between poetry and painting in their ability to create aesthetic imagery. This idea was first put forward by Su Shi in his "Notes to Wang Wei's Painting of *Mist and Rain over Languan*." Painting creates an aesthetic effect through images presented. Poetry, on the other hand, is a language art, which creates an aesthetic effect through the use of words. The former is an art that has shape but no sound, while the latter is an art that has sound but no shape. The term means that good poetry and painting should be fused so that a spontaneous and novel aesthetic realm can be created by a "picturesque poem" or a "poetic picture." This idea of Su Shi's had a far-reaching influence on the subsequent development of literature and painting in China.

CITATIONS

When reading Wang Wei's poems, one can conjure up a picturesque image. When viewing Wang Wei's paintings, one can experience a poetic sentiment. (Su Shi: *Dongpo's Comments on Literary and Artistic Works*)

Painting in poetry is a natural creation deriving from a poet's true aspiration; such poems cannot be composed by imitating others' paintings. Poetry in painting is inspired by a specific scene or sentiment at a given time, so it is not possible to artificially insert a poem into a painting. The way that a mind interacts with nature is as direct and unaffected as a life-like image reflected in a mirror. The effect is not deliberately intended at first. Nowadays, people do not understand this point. No wonder poetry and painting have become abused. (Shi Tao: *Dadizi's Comments on Paintings*)

166

shíshì-qiúshì
实事求是

Seek Truth from Facts

This term means handling things correctly according to realities of the situation. The term was originally used to describe the rigorous attitude of ancient Chinese scholars who paid great attention to acquiring solid facts in order to arrive at the correct understanding or conclusion. Later, it has come to mean expressing ideas or handling matters according to reality. It is a methodological principle on cognition and a fundamental principle underpinning behaviors and ethics. Basically, it calls for behaving in a practical, realistic, and honest way.

CITATION

Liu De, Prince Xian of Hejian... loved to study history and always sought the right understanding based on thorough grasp of evidence. (*The History of the Han Dynasty*)

167

sī

思

Reflecting / Thinking

The term means the ability to reflect and evaluate. Confucian scholars considered this a unique quality of the human mind. By reflecting, a person will keep himself from being led astray or getting confused by what he sees or hears. Through reflecting, a person will discover the foundation of morality. This leads to understanding natural laws, and eventually, the essence of being human. Without reflecting, humans will lose their individual consciousness and independence.

CITATIONS

Learning without reflecting leads to confusion; reflecting without learning leads to danger. (*The Analects*)

The eyes and ears cannot think, so they can be deceived or misled by external things. But the mind can think and reflect. Through reflection, cognition can be achieved, whereas without reflection nothing can be accomplished. This is the gift Heaven bestows on us. One should first establish the primacy of the mind, and then eyes and ears will not be misled. (*Mencius*)

168

sīwén

斯文

Be Cultured and Refined

Literally, the term means "this culture." It encompasses the cultural and ethical progress created by rites, music, education, codes, and systems as well as a social order which is hierarchical but harmonious. Later, this term came to refer to the literati and extended to mean being cultured and refined.

CITATION

If Heaven wished that this culture should perish, then I could do nothing about it. (*The Analects*)

169

sìduān
四端

Four Initiators

The four initiators are buds of four virtues: *ren* (仁), *yi* (义), *li* (礼), and *zhi* (智), or roughly benevolence, righteousness, propriety, and wisdom, which Mencius believed were all rooted in man's mind. Commiseration is the initiator of benevolence. Shame is the initiator of righteousness. Deference is the initiator of propriety and a sense of right and wrong is the initiator of wisdom. The four initiators are naturally possessed by man. They are fundamental features defining a human being. Man should fully cultivate and develop his inherent kindness, then he can accomplish the four virtues, and consequently become a man of virtue or even a sage.

CITATION

All who have the four initiators in them should know how to cultivate them, so that these initiators will grow, just like a fire that has started burning, or a spring that has started gushing out. If people can cultivate and expand the four initiators, they can bring stability to the world. Otherwise, they can hardly provide for their parents. (*Mencius*)

170

sìhǎi
四海

Four Seas

Four Seas refer to the territory of China or the entire world. The ancient Chinese believed that China was a land surrounded by Four Seas – the East, West, North, and South seas. The term suggests what the ancient Chinese conceived to be the map of China and the world: Nine *zhou* (regions) were located at the center of *tianxia* (all under heaven). *Tianxia* consisted of nine *zhou* and its surrounding Four Seas. China was within the Four Seas, while foreign lands were outside the Four Seas. In ancient China, Four Seas referred to all under heaven in most cases, and did not denote a specific body of water. Therefore, the term was used sometimes to mean the seas surrounding the land, and sometimes to specify the land surrounded by the Four Seas.

CITATION

A man of virtue always does things conscientiously without making any mistakes and treats people respectfully and appropriately. Then all within the Four Seas will be his brothers. (*The Analects*)

171

sìshū

四书

Four Books

This term refers collectively to the four Confucian classics: *The Analects, Mencius, The Great Learning,* and *The Doctrine of the Mean. The Great Learning* and *The Doctrine of the Mean* originally were two sections of *The Book of Rites,* but before the Tang Dynasty they did not attract much attention. Following the revival of Confucianism which began in the Tang and Song dynasties, through the advocacy of Han Yu and Li Ao of the Tang Dynasty, the Cheng brothers (Cheng Hao and Cheng Yi) and Zhu Xi of the Song Dynasty, *The Great Learning* and *The Doctrine of the Mean* were given new meaning. Their standing was gradually elevated, and they were regarded just as important as *The Analects* and *Mencius*. The four were then collectively known as the Four Books. *Commentaries on the Four Books,* written by Zhu Xi, established the dominant position of the Four Books, which formed the foundation for the neo-Confucian scholars of the Song and Ming dynasties. The Four Books became the source from which the neo-Confucian scholars drew inspiration to further their learning, and thus exerted a profound influence on the development of Confucianism.

CITATION

The principles in the Four Books, i.e., *The Great Learning, The Doctrine of the Mean, The Analects,* and *Mencius,* are illuminating and easy to follow. (*Classified Conversations of Master Zhu Xi*)

172

tǐ

体

Ti

Ti (体) has three different meanings in the study of literature, art, and aesthetics. First, it refers to features that distinguish one particular category, form, or literary school from others. These features represent the overall form and artistic characteristics, including the structure, content, language, style, and other essential elements. Second, it refers only to literary and artistic style, not their form or shape. Third, it refers to the basic literary and artistic form, i.e., the writing style and literary genre. Scholars of literary theory in different historical periods did not use the same standards to classify literary styles. For example, Xiao Tong of the Southern Dynasties classified literary and artistic works into 38 styles or categories in his *Literary Anthology*. There is a wide range of writing styles and literary genres in classical Chinese literature, each with its own style and writing requirements. The style of a literary work reflects the author's individual artistic temperament, and, sometimes, also the literary and artistic trend in a particular era. This term is often used together with the name of a person or a dynasty to describe literary and artistic features peculiar to a school of literature. Examples are the Sao Style (represented by the famous poem, *Li Sao*, written by renowned poet Qu Yuan), Tao Style (represented by poet Tao Yuanming), and Jian'an Style (named after the period of Jian'an during the Han Dynasty). The term is widely used in literary criticism and appreciation.

CITATIONS

People are always quick to see their own strengths. However, given the rich variety of literary styles, few people are accomplished in all of them. Therefore, people always write in the styles they are good at while taking lightly other people's works written in styles they happen to be weak in. (Cao Pi: *On Literary Classics*)

For more than 400 years from the Han Dynasty to the Wei Dynasty, numerous talented poets came to the fore, and the styles of poetry and essay writing went through three major transformations. (*The History of Song of the Southern Dynasties*)

173

tiānrén-héyī

天人合一

Heaven and Man Are United as One.

The term represents a world outlook and a way of thinking which hold that heaven and earth and man are interconnected. This world outlook emphasizes the integration and inherent relationship between heaven, earth, and man. It highlights the fundamental significance of nature to man or human affairs, and describes the endeavor made by man to pursue life, order, and values through interaction with nature. The term has different ways of expression in history, such as heaven and man are of the same category, sharing the same vital energy, or sharing the same principles. Mencius, for one, believed that through mental reflection one could gain understanding of human nature and heaven, emphasizing the unity of mind, human nature, and heaven. Confucian scholars of the Song Dynasty sought to connect the principles of heaven, human nature, and the human mind. Laozi maintained that "man's law is earthly, earth's law is natural, and heaven's law is Dao." Depending on a different understanding of heaven and man, the term may have different meanings.

CITATIONS

In terms of integration of categories, heaven and man are one. (Dong Zhongshu: *Luxuriant Gems of The Spring and Autumn Annals*)

A Confucian scholar is sincere because of his understanding, and he achieves understanding because of his sincerity. That is why heaven and man are united as one. One can become a sage through studies, and master heaven's law without losing understanding of man's law. (Zhang Zai: *Enlightenment Through Confucian Teachings*)

174

tiānrénzhīfēn

天人之分

Distinction Between Man and Heaven

This term refers to a world outlook and a way of thinking which hold that heaven and man are different. This explanation was first put forward by Xunzi, who did not believe that human morality and the order of human society emanated from heaven. He argued that heaven and man each had a different role and that they should not be mixed. Temporal changes of heaven and earth as well as the occurrence of seasonal changes in temperature and rainfall all belonged to the domain of heaven. They had their normal path, unrelated to human affairs, and were beyond the reach of human power. On the other hand, man's morality and order in the world belonged to the realm of man. People should be responsible for moral development and social order. Only by making a clear distinction between heaven and man could one develop his abilities on the basis established by heaven, without overstepping into a domain where man was unable to exert his power.

CITATION

Nature's ways are constant. They did not exist because Yao was on the throne or disappear because Jie was the ruler... When you work diligently in agriculture and are frugal in expenditures, nature cannot impoverish you. When you are well provided for with what you need and work at the proper time, nature cannot make you sick. When you firmly follow the right path, nature cannot bring you disaster... Therefore, he who understands the distinction between nature and man may be called the wisest man. (*Xunzi*)

175

tiānzǐ

天子

Son of Heaven

The Son of Heaven refers to the emperor or monarch, the supreme ruler of an empire or dynasty. People in ancient times believed that a monarch ruled the world by Heaven's decree and with its mandate, hence he was called the Son of Heaven. This term asserted that a ruler's authority was legitimate and sacred, as it was bestowed by Heaven, but to some extent, it also restricted the exercise of this power. This has some similarity to the Western concept of the divine right of kings by the grace of God, but there are fundamental differences. *Tian* (天), the Chinese word for Heaven, is not the same as the Western term "God." Rather, the Chinese term also implies the idea of interaction between Heaven and man, which means that the decree of Heaven also embodies popular will and popular support.

CITATIONS

So diligent is the Son of Heaven! His fame will forever be remembered. (*The Book of Songs*)

Therefore a man whose virtue is equal to that of heaven and earth can be an emperor. Heaven blesses him and takes him as his son, so he is called the Son of Heaven. (Dong Zhongshu: *Luxuriant Gems of The Spring and Autumn Annals*)

176

wēnróu-dūnhòu

温柔敦厚

Mild, Gentle, Sincere, and Broadminded

This term refers to the mild and broadminded manner with which the Confucian classic, *The Book of Songs*, edifies people. Confucian scholars during the Qin and Han dynasties believed that although some poems of *The Book of Songs* were satirical and remonstrative in tone, it still focused on persuading people instead of just reproving them. Most of the poems in the book were moderate in tone and meant to encourage the reader to learn to be moderate and honest. Encouraging people to be mild and gentle, sincere and broadminded is a manifestation of Confucian doctrine of the mean, and being fair and gentle is an aesthetic value, which is also a standard for literary and artistic style that stresses the need for being gentle in persuasion and for edification.

CITATIONS

When you enter a state, you can find out whether its people are proper in behavior. If they show themselves to be mild and gentle, sincere and broadminded, they must have learned it from *The Book of Songs*. (*The Book of Rites*)

Teaching people to be mild and gentle, sincere and broadminded is the basic purpose of *The Book of Songs*. One can write poetry with such characteristics only if one is endowed with such good qualities. (Zhu Tingzhen: *Xiaoyuan's Comments on Poetry*)

177

wénbǐ

文笔

Writing and Writing Technique

The term generally refers to different types of writings. Its meanings have evolved over time. During the Western and Eastern Han dynasties, it generally referred to writing techniques, writing styles, and various types of articles. During the Wei, Jin, and the Southern and Northern dynasties, literary scholars began to identify different features in different types of writings. They distinguished, for the first time, literary writings from those interpreting classical works, and identified pure literature as literary writings and practical writings as technical writings. They subsequently distinguished, on the basis of form, literary works such as poems, *fu* (赋 descriptive prose interspersed with verse), *song* (颂 verses in praise of merits and virtues), and *zan* (赞 mostly verses in praise of heroes) from essays such as memorials, documents, and policy proposals submitted to the emperor by officials. They concluded that all writings with rhyme were literary writings and those without were technical writings. Xiao Yi, Emperor Yuan of Liang, argued further that literary writings should not only have rhyme, but also express the author's inner feelings and use elaborate rhetoric, while technical writings required only general writing skills. Today, this term mainly refers to writing techniques and language styles.

CITATIONS

Writings without rhyme or rhythm are technical writings while those with rhyme and rhythm are literary ones. (Liu Xie: *The Literary Mind and the Carving of Dragons*)

Ambitious and studious from a young age, Xi Zaochi was an erudite scholar known for his writings and writing techniques. (*The History of the Jin Dynasty*)

178

wénxué

文学

Literature

Originally, the term meant to command a good knowledge of documents from previous dynasties. *Wen* (文) referred to documents, and *xue* (学) referred to the study of these documents. Later, the term referred to articles and documents in general as well as the knowledge about those documentations. The term had three main meanings. Firstly, from the pre-Qin period to the end of the Eastern Han Dynasty, it meant knowledge of ancient literature, especially that of humanities including poetry, history, rites and music, as well as works of laws and regulations. Starting from the Wei and Jin dynasties, the term basically became equivalent to today's concept of literature, but it also referred to academic writings on humanities. With the introduction of the Western concept of literature in recent history, the term gradually evolved to mean a pursuit that uses language to create aesthetic images. However, a few scholars, such as Zhang Taiyan, stuck to its traditional definition. The original meaning of the term determined the mainstream view on literature in contemporary China, which focuses on examining a literary phenomenon in the broader cultural context and emphasizing the intrinsic relationship between the aesthetic values of literature and liberal arts. This is somewhat different from the Western notion of literature which highlights the independent nature of literary appreciation. Secondly, the term refers broadly to various kinds of articles and documents in ancient times. Thirdly, it refers to scholars who promote learning through writing and teaching, as well as officials in charge of culture and education.

CITATIONS

Among the disciples of Confucius, Ziyou and Zixia have a good knowledge of ancient literature. (*The Analects*)

At that time, the Han Dynasty was on the rise, with Xiao He codifying laws, Han Xin promulgating military rules, Zhang Cang formulating the calendar and measurements, and Shusun Tong establishing ceremonial rites. Soon, literary talent who excelled in writing and learning took up positions in the imperial court. Lost classics such as *The Book of Songs* and *The Book of History* were rediscovered one after another. (*Records of the Historian*)

Generally speaking, Confucian studies are based on *The Book of Rites*, as exemplified by Xunzi. Historiography is modeled on *The Book of History* and *The Spring and Autumn Annals*, as exemplified by Sima Qian. Metaphysical studies are based on *The Book of Changes*, as exemplified by Zhuangzi. Literature has its root in *The Book of Songs*, as exemplified by Qu Yuan. (Liu Xizai: *Overview of Literary Theories*)

179

wénzhāng
文章

Literary Writing

The term refers to all kinds of writings, including what we call essays and books today. In the Pre-Qin period, this term was subsumed under literature. During the Han Dynasty, the term referred to writings other than *wenxue* (文学 documents of previous dynasties) to specifically mean essays, articles, history books, and treatises. In the Six Dynasties, the term, together with *wenxue,* began to assume the meaning of what later generations meant by literature, that is, writings for aesthetic appreciation which encompass every type of literary works. *Zhang* (章) also implies a movement of music played to its finish, or a single piece of music. Therefore, the term focuses on both meaning and structure as well as writing skills and techniques. Both Chinese characters in the term have the meaning of interwoven patterns and colors. Together, they signify a beautiful form, giving the term an aesthetic connotation. The earlier concept of the term is related to but different from that of *wenxue,* with the former focusing more on elegant diction and style, indicating increasing attention to the aesthetic value of literary works.

CITATIONS

Literary writings reflect one's moods and disposition, or give expression to one's inner world. Before writing, one should gather his thoughts and free his mind so as to transcend the limitations of time and space. Thus, once he starts writing, his work will achieve its flavor naturally. (*The History of Qi of the Southern Dynasties*)

Writings by sages in ancient times are all called "literary writings." Isn't this because they all have literary elegance? (Liu Xie: *The Literary Mind and the Carving of Dragons*)

180

Wú-Yuè-tóngzhōu
吴越同舟

People of Wu and Yue Are in the Same Boat.

In the Spring and Autumn Period, Wu and Yue were neighboring states which were hostile to each other. Wu and Yue people being in the same boat is a metaphor for overcoming old grievances to face common danger. When people from these two states were crossing a river in the same boat and encountered a storm, they had to work together to save themselves; in that sense, they were just like the left and right hands of the same person. The story implies that there is no absolute and perpetual enmity or friendship. Under certain circumstances, an enemy can be turned into a friend.

CITATION

People of the states of Wu and Yue were crossing a river in the same boat when they encountered strong winds and waves midstream. To save themselves from a common peril, they worked together like the left and right hands of the same person. (*Collected Works of the Confucian Family*)

181

wǔjīng

五经

Five Classics

The term refers to the five Confucian classics: *The Book of Songs, The Book of History, The Book of Rites, The Book of Changes,* and *The Spring and Autumn Annals.* In the pre-Qin period, the term "Six Classics" was used, referring to *The Book of Songs, The Book of History, The Book of Rites, The Book of Music, The Book of Changes,* and *The Spring and Autumn Annals. The Book of Music,* did not exist in written form, hence people often used the term "Five Classics" during the Han Dynasty. After Emperor Wu of the Han Dynasty established the title of "Academician of the Five Classics," study of these works became the foundation of Chinese learning, culture, and thought. In terms of content, the Five Classics each has its own focus; for instance, *The Book of Songs* deals with aspirations, and *The Book of History* chronicles events. Different in focus but complementing each other, they form an integral collection of classics. Throughout history, Confucian scholars added significant meaning to these classics with their interpretations of the original texts. The Five Classics comprise traditional Chinese culture's fundamental understanding of world order and values, epitomizing the concept of Dao.

CITATION

Which are the Five Classics? They are: *The Book of Songs, The Book of History, The Book of Rites, The Book of Changes,* and *The Spring and Autumn Annals.* (*Debates of the White Tiger Hall*)

182

xiāoyáo
逍遥

Carefree

The term refers to a state of mind totally free from all constraints. It was first proposed by Zhuangzi in one of his most well-known essays. According to him, people's minds can go beyond predicament in a way that their bodies cannot, so mentally they can be independent of material concerns and free of all worries. Guo Xiang of the Western Jin Dynasty had a new definition of the term: By acting in accordance with its own nature, everything can be free of troubles and worries.

CITATIONS

People should seek carefree enjoyment beyond the constraints of the human world. (*Zhuangzi*)

Things, big and small, are different from each other. But when they are placed where they should be, each of them will develop as its nature dictates, shoulder their proper responsibilities, and ultimately achieve the same degree of freedom. (Guo Xiang: *Annotations on Zhuangzi*)

183

xiǎorén

小人

Petty Man

The term was originally used to indicate a person's social status, usually referring to the rulers' subjects or those low in social ranking. Later generations also used the term to indicate one's moral standard in a disapproving way. Those of base character were called petty men as opposed to men of virtue. A petty man only pursues his personal interests or profits, even by violating morality and righteousness; and such people have no understanding of or regard for Dao.

CITATIONS

A man of virtue understands and observes what is morally right; while a petty man only has his eyes on and goes after what brings him personal gains. (*The Analects*)

They are petty men because they only seek ease and comfort of the moment and pursue personal gains. (Zhu Xi: *The Analects Variorum*)

184

xīngjì

兴寄

Xingji (Association and Inner Sustenance)

The term means the use of analogy, association, and inner sustenance in writing a poem to give implicit expression to one's sentiments, thus enabling the poem to convey a subtle message. The term was first used by the Tang-dynasty poet Chen Zi'ang. *Xing* (兴) means the development of inner feelings invoked by external objects, and *ji* (寄) means finding sustenance in them. Later it was extended to mean that poetry should be written to convey a message of praise or satire. The term carried on the pre-Qin poetical tradition of creating inspiration by writing about a subject and stressed that while depicting sentiments in poetry, the poet should find sustenance in it. The term represented an important development of the theory of analogy and association. It played a major role in ensuring that poets in the prime of the Tang Dynasty broke away from the poetic style of the Qi and Liang of the Southern Dynasties, which pursued ornate language instead of inner sustenance, thus enabling Tang poetry to develop in a healthy way.

CITATIONS

When I read the poems of the Qi and Liang of the Southern Dynasties in my leisure time, I found them full of ornate rhetoric heaped together without sustenance. I often feel resigned as I can well imagine that the ancients were always concerned about poetry becoming decadent and the tradition of objectively reflecting reality as shown in *The Book of Songs* getting lost. (Chen Zi'ang: Preface to My Poem "The Bamboo" Composed with Inspirations from Dongfang Qiu)

I was concerned that the works based on association and inner sustenance would get lost and that writings with only elaborate rhetoric would prevail. We really need works that have substance. (Liu Zongyuan: Letter to Scholar Shen Qi)

185

xīngqù

兴趣

Xingqu (Charm)

The term refers to charm inherent in an inspiration, or charm created when the object or scene depicted in a poem is appreciated. It is a type of aesthetic enjoyment contained in a poem which is gained through the reader's act of appreciation. In *Canglang's Criticism of Poetry,* Yan Yu, a poetry critic of the Southern Song Dynasty, voiced his love for poetry's emotional charm and argued against direct expression of an idea in poetry. He stressed the need to enable readers to gain insight and satisfaction in a natural way through personal reflection and contemplation. This term later became an important criterion for evaluating poetry, exerting a strong influence on the poetry theories of the Ming and Qing dynasties.

CITATIONS

One should write poetry only to express one's true sentiments and personality. In their poems, Tang-dynasty poets made particular efforts to inspire meaning, charm, and emotion. Their style is like an antelope hooking its horns onto a tree when sleeping at night, so that its trace cannot be found. (Yan Yu: *Canglang's Criticism of Poetry*)

Classical poems mostly focused on inspiring meaning, charm, and emotion through hints with subtle wording and implied meanings, and that is why they moved readers. Poets during the Song Dynasty, however, tended to use poetry to comment on public affairs or make arguments. If that was what they wanted to achieve, why didn't they write essays instead of poems? (Tu Long: On Essay Writing)

186

xíng'érshàng

形而上

What Is Above Form / The Metaphysical

The term means what is formless or has no formal substance yet. It generally indicates the basis of physical things. The term "what is above form" comes from *The Book of Changes* and is used as the opposite of "what is under form." "Form" indicates physical shape. "What is above form" refers to the state before a physical shape emerges, namely, formlessness. That which is formless is called "Dao."

CITATION

What is above form is called Dao, and what is under form is called "an object." (*The Book of Changes*)

187

xíng'érxià

形而下

What Is Under Form / The Physical

The term means what has a form or what has a formal substance. It generally indicates existing and concrete things. The term "what is under form" comes from The Book of Changes. It is used as the opposite of "what is above form." "Form" indicates physical shape. "What is under form" refers to the state after a physical shape has emerged, namely, physical existence. That which has a form is called "an object." What is under form takes what is above form as the basis of its existence.

CITATION

What is above form is called "Dao," and what is under form is called "an object." (*The Book of Changes*)

188

xūyī'érjìng

虚壹而静

Open-mindedness, Concentration, and Tranquility

This refers to a state of mind Xunzi proposed as a way to master the Dao of general morality. He believed that one gets to know Dao through the action of one's heart and mind. But since the human heart and mind are often closed, they can only function normally when one is open-minded, concentrated, and consequently tranquil. *Xu* (虚), or open-mindedness, prevents prior knowledge from hindering the acquisition of new knowledge. *Yi* (壹), or concentration, allows one to assimilate knowledge of different categories while keeping them from interfering with each other. *Jing* (静), or tranquillity, is to keep the false and confusing knowledge from obstructing one's normal process of contemplation.

CITATION

How can people learn to know Dao? The answer is to use one's heart and mind. How can the heart and mind know? The answer is to achieve open-mindedness, concentration, and tranquillity. (*Xunzi*)

189

xué

学

Learn

To Confucianism, learning is the way to cultivate oneself to achieve moral integrity. The usual meaning of the term is to acquire knowledge and understanding, but for Confucianism it focuses more on the cultivation of moral and ethical qualities to achieve personal growth. Through learning classics and rites, and following the practices of sages, a person is able to cultivate and improve his moral standards and thus become a person of ideal qualities. Daoists, on the other hand, are against learning, and Laozi said that "fine-sounding arguments" only cause unnecessary worries, and can disrupt a person's natural state of mind.

CITATIONS

Isn't it a pleasure to learn and apply from time to time what one has learned? (*The Analects*)

A man of virtue learns extensively, reflects upon and examines himself every day; he thus becomes wise and knowledgeable, and conducts himself properly. (*Xunzi*)

190

yǎngmín

养民

Nurturing the People

This term means to provide the people with necessities of life and educate them. According to *The Book of History*, this is what constitutes good governance. To reach this goal, the ruler must manage well the "six necessities and three matters," the six necessities being metal, wood, water, fire, land, and grain, and the three matters being fostering virtue, proper use of resources, and ensuring people's livelihood. This concept of governance, which focuses on promoting both economic and ethical progress, is people-centered.

CITATIONS

The king's virtue is reflected in good governance, which means to nurture the people. The people's need for water, fire, metal, wood, land, and grain must be well satisfied; and fostering virtue, proper use of resources, and ensuring people's well-being should be pursued in a coordinated way. When these nine things are accomplished in an orderly way, the king will win people's respect. (*The Book of History*)

Poverty stems from wealth, weakness from strength, turmoil from stability, and danger from security. Therefore, as he nurtures the people, a wise ruler cares about their sufferings, thanks them for their work, and teaches and instructs them so as to eradicate the seeds of evil no matter how tiny they might be. (Wang Fu: *Views of a Hermit*)

191

yìshù

艺术

Art

Originally, the term referred to six forms of classical arts and various crafts, but it later extended to include artistic creation and aesthetic appreciation. The six forms of arts as defined by Confucianism are poetry, writing, rites, music, archery, and driving horse-pulled carriages. These constituted the basic requirements for cultivating a man of virtue. These six arts also included what later generations deemed as arts. Sometimes, the term also meant the six classics, namely, *The Book of Songs, The Book of History, The Book of Rites, The Book of Changes, The Book of Music,* and *The Spring and Autumn Annals.* Zhuangzi, on his part, emphasized the connection between crafts and arts, regarding them as physical and mental creative activities that help one gain insight into Dao. The various ideas about arts put forward by Confucian, Daoist, and Buddhist scholars defined the nature and method of Chinese arts, which seek unity between artwork and real life, fusion of senses and experiences, and integration of techniques and personality, with achieving artistic conception as the ultimate aim. Since the introduction of Western art theories in modern China, arts have become an independent discipline covering all types of arts created with skill and innovation. The concept of arts today incorporate both traditional Chinese and contemporary Western notions of arts.

CITATIONS

A man of virtue pursues Dao, practices virtue and benevolence, and engages extensively in six arts. (*The Analects*)

Arts refer to such basic skills required by the six classics, arithmetic, archery, and driving horse-pulled carriages. Crafts refer to such professions as medicine, fortune-telling, divination, and necromancy. (*The History of the Later Han Dynasty*)

Fortune-telling has a long history. In ancient times, kings used fortune-telling to make decisions, weigh consequences, foresee fate, and judge outcomes. (*The History of the Jin Dynasty*)

192

yìjìng
意境

Aesthetic Conception

The term refers to a state where the scene described in a literary or artistic work reflects the sense and sensibility intended. *Jing* (境) originally meant perimeter or boundary. With the introduction of Buddhism into China during the late Han, Wei and Jin dynasties, the idea gained popularity that the physical world was but an illusion, and that only the mind was real in existence. So *jing* came to be seen as a realm that could be attained by having sensibilities of the mind. As a literary and artistic term, *jing* has several meanings. The term *yijing* (意境) was originally put forward by renowned Tang poet Wang Changling. It describes an intense aesthetic experience in which one's perception of an object reaches a realm of perfect union with the implication denoted by the object. Aesthetic appreciation in the mind is characterized by "projecting meaning into a scene" and "harmonizing one's thought with a scene." In contrast with the term *yixiang* (意象), *yijing* (意境) fully reveals the implication and the heightened aesthetic sense that an artistic work is intended to deliver. The concept is extended to include other notions such as sentiment and scene, actual and implied meanings, or mind and object. It also raises literary and artistic works to a new realm of aesthetic appreciation. After evolving through several dynasties, this concept developed into an important criterion to judge the quality of a literary or artistic work, representing an accomplishment drawing on classical writings through ages. It has also become a hallmark for all outstanding literary and artistic works. The term also represents a perfect union between foreign thoughts and culture and those typically Chinese.

CITATIONS

A poem accomplishes aesthetic conception in three ways. The first is through objects. If you want to write poems about landscape, you need to observe intensely springs and creeks, rocks and towering peaks, imprint their extraordinary beauty and charm on your memory, put yourself in the scene created in your mind, and view in your mind's eye the image you obtain until you can see it as vividly as if it were right on your palm. By then, you can start to think about writing the poem. A deep appreciation of the scene and its objects is instrumental in achieving a true poetic image. The second is through sentiments. Sentiments such as happiness, pleasure, sorrow, and anger should be allowed to develop in your mind. You should experience them personally to fully grasp the nature of these emotions. This will enable you to express them in a profound way. The third is through an imagined scene. This requires you to reach aesthetic appreciation by reflecting it in your mind time and again. Then you can capture the genuine nature of an idea. (Wang Changling: *Rules of Poetry*)

A beautifully composed poem is one in which the blending of image and concept is such that it transcends that of sound and music. Only then can one savor the real charm of poetry. (Zhu Chengjue: *Comments on the Collection of Poems from Cunyutang Study*)

Poems have limited verse forms and rhythmic patterns, but we poets are capable of creating fresh ideas every day, all the time. (Zhou Bingzeng: Preface to *Collection of Poems from Daoyuantang Study*)

193

yìxīng
意兴

Inspirational Appreciation

The term refers to the meaning implicit in an inspiration, or meaning and charm generated when poetic emotion encounters an external object or scene. It is an artistic image an author creates when appreciating the beauty and charm intrinsic in an object or scene. According to this term, an author should incorporate his sentiments and thoughts into the object or scene depicted to convey them through artistic images and aesthetic appreciation. This will spark the reader's imagination and thus enable him to gain a deeper appreciation of a poem.

CITATIONS

A good poem instills meaning and inspiration in its description of scenery and imagery. If a poem only describes scenery and fails to inspire people, no matter how eloquent the description may be, it will have little appeal. (Wang Changling: *Rules of Poetry*)

Poets of the Southern Dynasties were good at using rhetoric but weak in logic. The poets of our Song Dynasty champion logic but are weak in creating inspirational ideas. Poets of the Tang Dynasty gave equal weight to both meaning and inspiration, with logic implicit in both. The poems of the Han and Wei dynasties blended the choice of words, logic, and the inspiration imperceptibly. (Yan Yu: *Canglang's Criticism of Poetry*)

194

yǔzhòu

宇宙

Universe / Cosmos

The original meaning of the term is the eave and beam of a house, while its extended meaning is time and space as well as the whole world composed of limitless time and space. The first character *yu* (宇) means heaven and earth as well as all the directions of north, south, east, west, the above, and the below. The second character *zhou* (宙) means all of time, the past, present, and future. Together, the term means infinite space and endless time. In Chinese philosophy, "theories of the universe" are concerned with the existence of the world in an ontological sense, and with its process of evolution.

CITATIONS

The past, present, and future are called *zhou*; north, south, east, west, the above, and the below are called *yu*. (*Huainanzi*)

Yu means space without limit; *zhou* represents time without end. (Zhang Heng: *Law of the Universe*)

195

yuán

元

Yuan (Origin)

The term means the primal source from which all things originate, both animate and inanimate, including human beings. *Yuan* (元) manifests itself in different forms. In the Han Dynasty, it was considered a kind of primal physical material that both produced and made up the myriad things of the world. *The Book of Changes* divides *yuan* into two primal sources: the heavenly source which gives birth to the sun, moon, and stars, and the earthly source which creates all other things on earth. In *The Spring and Autumn Annals*, the term refers to the first year in its chronologies, symbolizing the start of a new historical period, and serving as the manifestation in the human world of the natural process in which things begin, end, and are replaced.

CITATIONS

Yuan is a vital force, without shape in the beginning. It then takes on form to create both heaven and earth, and is the source of all their transformations. (He Xiu: *Annotations on Gongyang' s Commentary on The Spring and Autumn Annals*)

Great is the *qian* hexagram! All things owe their existence to it, and it guides the movement of heaven and creates its impact. (*The Book of Changes*)

Why does *The Spring and Autumn Annals* give such importance to *yuan*? This is because *yuan* is the primordial source of all things. (Dong Zhongshu: *Luxuriant Gems of The Spring and Autumn Annals*)

196

zhèngzhì

政治

Decree and Governance / Politics

The term has two meanings. First, it refers to all measures for governing a country. *Zheng* (政) stands for decrees, rules, and ordinances, and *zhi* (治) refers to their implementation, that is, the way in which the people are governed. Second, it refers to a state of stable and sound governance of the country, with an efficient and clean government, a prosperous economy, and a peaceful society. In modern times, the term is used in the sense of "politics," as it refers to policies, measures, and actions that governments, political parties, social groups, or individuals adopt in domestic or international affairs.

CITATIONS

Shaping people's mind through popularizing education and exercising good governance will benefit the people. (*The Book of History*)

Decrees are adopted to maintain public order, while punishments are meted out to eliminate evil. (*Zuo's Commentary on The Spring and Autumn Annals*)

197

zhīxíng
知行

Knowledge and Application

"Knowledge" refers to awareness and examination of the principles underlying human relations in everyday life, and "application" refers to the implementation of these principles in everyday life. "Knowledge and application," used in ancient China, were not in the general sense of having knowledge of external objects, or taking action to utilize and transform external things. Rather, they were recognition and application of principles underlying human relations in everyday life. One acquires "knowledge" in different ways: through visual perception, hearing, or mental reflection and insight. Some people think that "knowledge" is difficult and that "application" is easy. Some think that "knowledge" is easy and that "application" is difficult. Some think that "knowledge" and "application" are equally difficult. As for the relationship between "knowledge" and "application", some maintain that knowledge and application are united as one. Others think that knowledge and application are separate. These varied understanding of "knowledge and application" determine different ways of fostering virtue and of instruction concerning human relations.

CITATIONS

To know is not the hard part; to apply is. (*Zuo's Commentary on The Spring and Autumn Annals*)

Not having heard something is not as good as having heard it; having heard it is not as good as having seen it; having seen it is not as good as knowing it; knowing it is not as good as putting it into practice. Learning reaches the ultimate stage when it is being applied. (*Xunzi*)

198

zhǐgēwéiwǔ

止戈为武

Stopping War Is a True Craft of War.

To be able to stop war is a true craft of war. This famous military view was first raised by King Zhuang of Chu in the Spring and Autumn Period, on the basis of the structure of the Chinese character *wu* (武). *Wu* is composed of *zhi* (止), which means to stop; and *ge* (戈), which means dagger-axe or weapons and is used here in the metaphorical sense of warfare. To interpret *wu* as stopping war was consistent with the cultural characteristics of Chinese characters. It also expresses the Chinese people's thinking of using military means to stop violence and their love of peace and opposition to war.

CITATION

When Cang Jie created Chinese script, he put *zhi* (止 stop) and *ge* (戈 dagger-axe) together to make *wu* (武 war). To stop war, sages used military force to quell violence and turmoil. They did not abuse their military power to commit atrocities of killing and destroying their opponents. (*The History of the Han Dynasty*)

199

zìqiáng-bùxī
自强不息

Striving Continuously to Strengthen Oneself

The term means that one should strive continuously to strengthen himself. Ancient Chinese believed that heavenly bodies move in accordance with their own nature in a vigorous and forever forward-going cycle. A man of virtue, who follows the law of heaven, should be fully motivated and work diligently to strengthen himself. This is the Chinese view on governance and self development, established with reference to the movement of heavenly bodies. Together with the notion that a true gentleman has ample virtue and carries all things, it constitutes the fundamental trait of the Chinese nation.

CITATIONS

Just as heaven keeps moving forward vigorously, a man of virtue should strive continuously to strengthen himself. (*The Book of Changes*)

Neither monarchs, ministers, nor commoners have ever achieved great accomplishments in the world without first striving to strengthen themselves. (*Huainanzi*)

Facing hostile countries, we must first of all strive to become strong. If we have strengthened ourselves, enemy states will fear us and we will not fear them. (*The History of the Song Dynasty*)

200

zǒngjí
总集

General Collection / Anthology

Zongji (总集) is a collection of various authors' poems and proses (distinct from *bieji* [别集], a collection of a particular author's literary works). The earliest anthology we find nowadays is *Verses from the Odes of Chu*, compiled and edited by Wang Yi in the Han Dynasty. In terms of content, an anthology could be either comprehensive or limited in selection. Chronically, an anthology can be a general collection spanning written history, or a general collection from one dynasty. In terms of the genre of collected works, it can be divided into collections of a specific genre and collections of various genres. The most representative anthology is *Selected Literary Works* compiled and edited jointly by Crown Prince Xiao Tong and his literary advisors in the Liang Dynasty of the Southern Dynasties. *Selected Literary Works* consists of more than 700 outstanding literary pieces of various genres from pre-Qin through the early Liang. It does not include any work that belongs to the categories of *jing* (经 Confucian classics), *shi* (史 history), or *zi* (子 thoughts of ancient scholars and schools), but does include a small number of prefaces, commentaries, and eulogies from *shi*. *Selected Literary Works* reflects the literary trend of the time and exerted a far-reaching impact on the development of Chinese literature in the years to come.

CITATIONS

An anthology was compiled because a large number of works of *ci* (辞) and *fu* (赋) were created, and different collections of various authors were widespread. They were put together under the title of *Literary Trends and Schools* by Zhi Yu of the Jin Dynasty. (*The History of the Sui Dynasty*)

The form of anthology originated from *The Book of History* and *The Book of Songs*. After *Verses from the Odes of Chu* and *Literary Trends and Schools* were compiled and edited by Wang Yi and Zhi Yu respectively, various anthologies began to appear, and became clear in themes and formats. (Ma Qichang: Preface to *Selected Classic Works of the Tongcheng School*)

PART III

201

báimiáo

白描

Plain Line Drawing

Plain line drawing is one of the traditional Chinese styles of artistic presentation. It features the contours of images sketched in black ink lines. This style of painting is mostly used in painting human figures and flowers. Although not much ink is applied, this technique can achieve a very lively effect. Plain line drawing originated from the plain drawing of earlier times; through variations in lines' length, thickness, pressure, and changes in trajectory, the artist can portray the texture and motion of images. Plain line drawing was prevalent from the Jin Dynasty through the Tang Dynasty. During the Song Dynasty, it formed a distinctive style of its own. Gu Kaizhi of the Jin Dynasty, Li Gonglin of the Northern Song Dynasty, and Zhao Mengfu of the Yuan Dynasty specialized in painting lines of perfectly even width like iron wire, while Wu Daozi of the Tang Dynasty and Ma Hezhi of the Southern Song Dynasty were renowned for their skill in drawing thick, wavy lines resembling orchid leaves. Plain drawing is also a very important style of expression in narrative literature. In this context it refers to a simple and concise style of writing, without embellishment, so as to produce fresh, lively images. In classic novels such as *Outlaws of the Marsh* or *Romance of the Three Kingdoms*, one finds abundant instances of a plain drawing style of writing.

CITATION

Paintings drawn with plain lines are prone to being overly fine or weak, often lacking a soaring spirit and vigor despite a feminine beauty. But today, after admiring this particular painting, I have found its strokes to be vigorous like bent wire. (When it comes to vigorous brushwork,) Yan Liben of the Tang Dynasty, Li Gonglin of the Northern Song Dynasty, and Zhao Mengfu of the Yuan Dynasty were truly a Great Triad. (Wang Zhideng: Postscript to *Korimaro Preaches a Sermon*)

202

biànhuà

变化

Change

The term refers to the fundamental state of the existence of things. *Bian* (变) and *hua* (化) may be used as one word or separately. Specifically, *bian* means manifest change, while *hua* indicates subtle and gradual change. Ancient Chinese thinkers generally held that all things under heaven and on earth, including humans and society, are all in a state of change. Only through constant change can they permanently exist and develop. Change is caused by constant clash and integration between the conflicting properties with which people and things are endowed. Some scholars believed that change follows a constant law and can thus be understood and grasped, while others maintained that change is unpredictable and therefore difficult to grasp. Buddhism, on the other hand, holds that changes of things are only superficial, and that all things are still and motionless.

CITATIONS

The interaction between firmness and gentleness produces change. (*The Book of Changes*)

Bian refers to obvious changes of things, while *hua* suggests gradual changes of things. (Zhang Zai: *Zhang Zai's Explanation of The Book of Changes*)

203

chényù

沉郁

Melancholy

Melancholy refers to an artistic style in poetic works in which sentiment expressed is subtle and the message is profound. Ancient Chinese poets represented by Du Fu, keenly concerned about state affairs and people's hardships, tried hard to understand what caused the rise and fall of a nation and sought ways to save the country and the people, but all to no avail. Such frustration and disappointment are thus reflected in their poems. With meticulously crafted structure, rhythm, and tones, their works give readers a special aesthetic appreciation of melody and infinite afterthought.

CITATION

Melancholy means that as a writer has given so much thought to the theme before writing, his work, once completed, contains profound sentiments beyond description. (Chen Tingzhuo: *Remarks on Lyrics from White Rain Studio*)

204

chéngyì
诚意

Be Sincere in Thought

The pursuit of moral principles in daily life should be true and sincere. "Being sincere in thought" is one of the "eight essential principles" from the philosophical text *The Great Learning*, the other seven being "studying things," "acquiring knowledge," "rectifying one's mind," "cultivating oneself," "regulating one's family well," "governing the state properly," and "bringing peace to all under heaven." Those constitute important stages in the moral cultivation advocated by Confucian scholars. "Sincerity in thought" has as its preceding stage the "extension of knowledge." One can only identify and follow the principle of "sincerity in thought" on the basis of understanding the moral principles in daily life. One's true desire will then naturally reflect itself in one's daily behavior. An individual's moral conduct must stem from a genuine wish and must not just conform superficially to the moral principles without true intention of practicing them.

CITATIONS

Being sincere in one's thought is to tolerate no self-deception, as one hates undesirable smells or likes lovely colors. That is what is called satisfied with oneself. (*The Book of Rites*)

Being sincere in thought is of primary importance in self-cultivation. (Zhu Xi: *Annotations on The Great Learning*)

205

chūnqiū

春秋

The Spring and Autumn Annals / The Spring and Autumn Period

The Spring and Autumn Annals is one of the Confucian classics, believed to have been compiled by Confucius based on the chronicles of the State of Lu. The book covers a period of 242 years from the first year of the reign of Duke Yin of Lu (722 BC) to the 14th year of the reign of Duke Ai (481 BC). The book was China's first chronological history, and its title has come to mean all chronological histories. Its records of events are brief and its style is concise. Later Confucian scholars regarded the book as having "subtle words with profound meanings," and described its implied and indirect style of writing, which makes both positive and negative criticism, as "*The Spring and Autumn Annals* style." *Zuo's Commentary on The Spring and Autumn Annals*, *Gongyang's Commentary on The Spring and Autumn Annals*, and *Guliang's Commentary on The Spring and Autumn Annals*, together known as the "Three Commentaries," are explications of this work. (Gongyang's and Guliang's commentaries explain the reasoning in the book, while Zuo's commentary records historical events of this period but does not interpret *The Spring and Autumn Annals*.) "Spring and Autumn" also refers to the Spring and Autumn Period, an era named after *The Spring and Autumn Annals*. There are two views about the period it spans: One is the period covered in the *Annals*, the other is the period from 770 BC, when King Ping of Zhou moved his capital from near present-day Xi'an in the west to present-day Luoyang in the east, until the year of 476 BC.

CITATIONS

Therefore the noble man said, "The style of *The Spring and Autumn Annals* is implicit but the meaning of the book is clear; it records both events and their profound significance. It is subtle yet logical, thorough yet not verbose. It chastises evil deeds and urges people to do good deeds. Who but a sage could have compiled this?" (*Zuo's Commentary on The Spring and Autumn Annals*)

Social mores and moral conduct were in decline; evil theories and violent deeds kept emerging; some subjects killed their rulers and some sons killed their fathers. Deeply worried, Confucius compiled *The Spring and Autumn Annals.* (*Mencius*)

206

cí
词

Ci (Lyric)

Ci (词) originated in the Tang and the Five Dynasties, and developed to maturity as a new literary form in the Song Dynasty. Also known as "lyric with a melody," "*yuefu* (乐府) poetry" or "long and short verses," *ci* developed from poetry. Its main feature is that it is set to music and sung. Each piece of *ci* has a name for its tune. There are strict requirements for the number of lines and the number of characters as well as tone pattern and rhyming in different tunes. In terms of length, *ci* is divided into short lyrics, medium lyrics, and long lyrics. In terms of musical system, a piece of *ci* is usually divided into two stanzas of *que* (阕) or *pian* (片), as ancient Chinese called them. Occasionally, it consists of three or four stanzas, or just one. Thus, the music can be played once or many times. In terms of style, *ci* falls into the graceful and restrained school and the bold and unconstrained school. The former is delicate and sentimental, often describing family life and love, while the latter is bold and free, often expressing one's vision about major social issues like the fate of the nation. Many literati and scholars of the Song Dynasty composed *ci* lyrics, which played a significant part in promoting its development. Today, *ci* is generally not set to music and sung. Rather, it is a literary form composed in accordance with the requirements of a music tune.

CITATIONS

Ci means lyrics written for music, whereas *qu* is musical tunes set to accompany lyrics. (Liu Xizai: *Overview of Literary Theories*)

During the Song and Yuan dynasties, *ci* and *qu* were one and the same thing. When written with words, they were *ci*; when composed with music, they were *qu*. (Song Xiangfeng: *Epilogue to Yuefu Poetry*)

207

cíqǔ
词曲

Ci (Lyric) and *Qu* (Melody)

Ci (词 a form of poetry with long or short verses which can be set to music and sung) and *qu* (曲 a form of rhyming compositions which can be set to music and sung) are a combined appellation for two kinds of literary styles. In the *Complete Library of the Four Branches of Literature,* they are listed at the very end of the "Collections" section (*Qu* is a sub-genre and is not listed in the table of contents). This is because according to the literary views of ancient scholars, poetry and essays were the only accepted tradition to express important ideas. To write in the form of *ci* (lyric) and *qu* (melody) was only seen as a minor skill showing a person's talent. Sometimes, the combined appellation *ciqu* also refers to traditional opera and genres of performances featuring speaking and singing.

CITATION

Ci and *qu* are genres falling between essay and performing skills. They are not highly regarded, and even their authors do not prize them. They are no more than rhetoric with which people show off their literary talent to each other! (*Complete Library of the Four Branches of Literature*)

208

cuòcǎi-lòujīn
错彩镂金

Gilded and Colored, Elegant and Refined

The term is used to describe an excessively exquisite artistic work as if it were an object painted in bright colors and inlaid with gold and silver. In the literary context, it refers to poems written in a highly rhetorical style. Aesthetically, what is "gilded and colored, elegant and refined" is considered undesirable, and the style of "lotus rising out of water" is preferred. The former focuses only on external form and appearance, whereas the latter, as a natural presentation of aesthetic ideas, penetrates appearances and brings out the essence.

CITATIONS

Yan Yanzhi asked Bao Zhao, "Whose works are better, mine or Xie Lingyun's?" Bao said, "Xie's five-word-to-a-line poems are as natural and lovely as lotus having just risen out of water in bloom, while yours are like embroidery embellished with colored decorations." (*The History of the Southern Dynasties*)

Red lacquer needs no decorated patterns, white jade needs no carving, and precious pearls need no adornment. Why? Because they are too good to be worked on. (Liu Xiang: *Garden of Stories*)

209

dàdào-zhìjiǎn

大道至简

Great Truth in Simple Words

The most popular and most fundamental truths, principles, and methodologies tend to be expressed in simple words and are easy to understand. *Dadao* (大道) means great truth, or universally applicable laws governing nature and society, or the fundamental principles for people to follow in treating nature and governing society. The Chinese character *jian* (简) means simple, concise, and easy. The term is often used to describe the governance of a state and management of society. It has two primary meanings. First, it means that the most popular and fundamental truths should be expressed in simple words so that ordinary people can easily understand and put them into practice. Second, *dadao* is not something separate and far away from reality. Rather, it is a practical ethical principle which is easy for people to follow in their daily lives. As long as one sees through the seemingly complicated superficialities and traces the source of things, one will be able to grasp the fundamental truths, discover the basic rules, and comprehend them in spite of the complexity.

CITATIONS

He is able to keep himself to the right path if he has an excellent command of extensive literary knowledge, constrains himself with ritual propriety, and starts from the most obvious point to arrive at the most convenient situation. (Zhang Zai: *Enlightenment Through Confucian Teachings*)

All great truths are most plain and easy to understand and most common in people's everyday life... as such, people do not think them as truths. (Yang Jian: *Cihu's Commentary on The Book of Songs*)

The Book of Changes is boundless and limitless, through the ever changing nature it offers. The reason why *The Book of Changes* offers infinite changes is attributable to the two kinds of *qi*: yin and yang. The reason why everything can be traced to the two kinds of *qi*, yin and yang, is that the theory of yin and yang is easy to understand and implement. (Xiang Anshi: *Expounding the Theories of The Book of Changes*)

210

dàqiǎo-ruòzhuō

大巧若拙

Exquisite Skill Looks Simple and Clumsy.

The term means that ingenuity and skill at their best look simple and clumsy. The greatest ingenuity should be something completely natural and that it has not been painstakingly worked on. The term comes from the book *Laozi*. Laozi the philosopher believed that everything should be in keeping with nature. He advocated non-action and was against any form of excessive act. Later, the term came to mean the highest possible level of skill and perfection in artistic and literary creation. In Chinese literary theory, "exquisite skill looks simple and clumsy" does not mean the clumsier the better, nor is it a rejection of skill. Rather, it rejects excessive embellishment and over-pursuit of the exquisite, and encourages well-founded simplicity and naturalness. The phrase represents the highest possible level of perfection in artistic beauty and skill and is also what the people in pre-modern China strove to achieve in calligraphy, painting, gardening, and other forms of art.

CITATION

Straightness, when extreme, looks crooked. Skill, when superb, looks clumsy. Eloquence, when great, seems to stammer. (*Laozi*)

211

dàtǐ, xiǎotǐ

大体、小体

The Major Organ and the Minor Organs

Referring to the heart and the sensory organs, this term was used by Mencius to differentiate between men of virtue and petty men. Sensory organs such as the ears and eyes are called "minor organs" because they lack a capacity for thought and for cognition, and are hence easily directed by externalities when they come into contact with the latter. If a man were to only rely on his "minor organs," he would be a captive of material desires and therefore become a petty man. The heart is the "major organ" which is naturally endowed with the capacity for thought and cognition. If a man is able to establish a dominant role for his "major organ," then through the actions of his heart, he will be able to continually increase its inherent goodness and not have his judgment clouded by material desires, and thereby become a man of virtue.

CITATION

Gongduzi asked, "We are all humans, so why are some men of virtue while others are petty men?" Mencius replied, "Those who follow their major organ become men of virtue, while those who follow their minor organs become petty men." (*Mencius*)

212

dàyòng

大用

Maximal Functioning

Maximal functioning means that all kinds of appearances of Dao in the external world are the greatest manifestation and functioning of Dao. Daoist scholars believe that the internal Dao determines the basis for changes in the external world, and that all kinds of forms in the objective world derive from the active, innate nature of Dao, the result of unity of substance and function. In "Twenty-four Styles of Poetry," Sikong Tu, a literary critic in the Tang Dynasty, made this notion a term of literary criticism to highlight the view that the rich and colorful imagery in poetry represents unity of the internal spirit of the work and its external shape. In poetry writing and appreciation, one should focus on the harmony between the appearance and the essence.

CITATION

The grand appearance is an external manifestation of Dao, while the true vitality permeates itself internally. Reverting to a tranquil void, one may gain fullness and amass inner strength, and he will produce powerful works. (Sikong Tu: Twenty-four Styles of Poetry)

213

dānqīng
丹青

Painting in Colors

Dan (丹 cinnabar) and *qing* (青 cyan) were two colors frequently applied in traditional Chinese painting. Cinnabar is red and cyan is bluish green. In early times, Chinese paintings often used minerals such as cinnabar and cyan to draw lines or fill in colors. Hence the term *danqing* (丹青) made from the combination of *dan* and *qing* could stand for painting in general. Representative works of this kind included silk paintings unearthed at Tomb No.1 of Mawangdui of the Han Dynasty as well as the Dunhuang frescoes of the Northern Wei period and the Sui and Tang dynasties. Later, colors made from cinnabar and cyan were gradually replaced by ink and wash. Partly because of their bright, contrastive colors, and partly because mineral colors do not deteriorate appreciably over time, people used red-character books to record merits and bluish-green-character books to record historical events. Historians often use *danqing* to refer to a man's outstanding, indelible work that deserves to be put down in history.

CITATIONS

Gu Kaizhi was particularly skillful in painting. The figures he portrayed are amazingly vivid and lovely. Xie An held him in high esteem, and regarded him as superior to all other artists, past and present. (*The History of the Jin Dynasty*)

Thus a painter portrays a person's physical features, just as a historian records his accomplishments. (Cao Pi: A Letter to Meng Da)

214

dànbó
淡泊

Quiet Living with No Worldly Desire

This term was first used to mean to lead a quiet, peaceful life with few worldly desires. Daoism advocates blandness, believing that lack of flavor is the best possible flavor. It was highly influential in the creation of the aesthetic concept of blandness and quiet living. Beginning in the Wei and Jin dynasties, the term was used in aesthetics, referring to a peaceful and mild artistic beauty and style, as opposed to rich, loud and splendid beauty. The term does not mean insipid with no taste at all; what it refers to is a purified, refined, quiet and unstrained taste, a mild yet profound tone and flavor.

CITATIONS

In conducting himself, a man of virtue should maintain inner peace to cultivate his moral character and be frugal to cultivate virtue. Unless he is indifferent to fame and fortune, he cannot have aspirations; unless he stays calm and quiet, he cannot reach afar. (Zhuge Liang: Letter of Warning to My Son)

Only Wei Yingwu and Liu Zongyuan outdid others in pursuing profound aspirations while leading a simple and unsophisticated life and in working for worthy goals while living a quiet life with no worldly desires. (Su Shi: Postscript to *Selected Poems of Huang Zisi*)

215

dànbó-míngzhì, níngjìng-zhìyuǎn
淡泊明志，宁静致远

Indifference to Fame and Fortune Characterizes a High Aim in Life, and Leading a Quiet Life Helps One Accomplish Something Lasting.

This saying, with the attitude to fame and fortune at its core, refers to a way in which people in ancient China sought to practice self-cultivation. People should not be greedy for fame and fortune and be burdened by such greed. Instead they ought to cherish noble ideals and work heart and soul to achieve them.

CITATIONS

Hence, unless he is indifferent to fame and fortune, he cannot demonstrate his virtue; unless he stays calm and quiet, he cannot reach afar; unless he is magnanimous, he cannot learn from others and be inclusive; unless he is kind and warm-hearted, he cannot embrace the people; unless he is even-handed and righteous, he cannot take control and make decisions. (*Huainanzi*)

Unless he is indifferent to fame and fortune, he cannot have aspirations; unless he stays calm and quiet, he cannot reach afar. (Zhuge Liang: Letter of Warning to My Son)

216

dāngháng

当行

Professionalism

The expression was first used in poetry criticism to mean that a poem fully met poetic stylistic standards. It later became an important term in Chinese classical operatic theory. It has two meanings. One is that the language used by a character in a play is simple, natural, easy to understand, and appropriate for the character. The other is that characters and plot of the play are true to life with a strong artistic attraction. In Ming-dynasty operatic theory, "professionalism" and "being true to life" are often used together to describe outstanding opera works.

CITATIONS

Beginning in the Yuan Dynasty, professional simplicity, rather than flowery rhetoric, has gained popularity as an operatic style. (Ling Mengchu: Miscellaneous Notes on Opera)

Professional actors can play their roles so vividly as if they were the characters themselves, forgetting that the story is fictional. Their performances can make viewers so happy that their beards will fly up, or make them so angry that they will wring their wrists, or make them so sad that they will sob, or inspire them so much that they will become thrilled. Only artists like Youmeng can create such effect. Therefore, for an opera to be outstanding, it first and foremost must be professional. (Zang Maoxun: Second Foreword to *Selected Works of Yuan Opera*)

217

dàojìtiānxià
道济天下

Support All People by Upholding Truth and Justice

The term means to save and help all people through upholding truth and justice. *Dao* (道) here refers to truth and justice, and also to particular thought or doctrine. *Ji* (济) means relieving or helping people out of difficulties or sufferings. *Tianxia* (天下) refers to everything under heaven, and particularly all people. Therefore, this phrase contains two meanings. First, the value of any particular Dao depends on whether it serves the interests of the people. Second, people of virtue, and intellectuals in particular, should apply Dao they have learned to serve the people and use the ancient classics they have studied to meet present needs. Much like the idea of "studying ancient classics to meet present needs," this notion of "supporting all people by upholding truth and justice," represents the ultimate goal and ideal character of the traditional Chinese intellectuals in their pursuit of knowledge. It also embodies the compassion and moral standards of the traditional Chinese intellectuals as they pursue and uphold truth, care about the livelihood of the people, and take upon themselves the responsibility for the world.

CITATIONS

Sages won't make mistakes, for they have endless wisdom about everything under heaven and their virtues help all people in the world. (*The Book of Changes*)

Han Yu's essays revitalized the style of writing that had been on the decline in the previous eight dynasties; his advocacy of Confucianism saved the people who had indulged themselves; his loyalty offended and enraged the emperor; and his courage could overawe the commander-in-chief of the armed forces. (Su Shi: Monument for the Temple of Han Yu in Chaozhou)

218

dédào-duōzhù, shīdào-guǎzhù

得道多助，失道寡助

A Just Cause Enjoys Abundant Support While an Unjust Cause Finds Little Support.

The Chinese phrase *dedao* (得道) or "obtaining Dao" here refers to having "a just cause." Since ancient times Chinese people have had a high esteem for justice and have thought of justice as a decisive factor determining success or failure in war and other enterprises. Only by upholding justice can one achieve internal unity and popular support, which are essential for the success of a war or a cause; otherwise, popular support is lost and the ruler or leader becomes too isolated and helpless to succeed. This is a specific expression of the Chinese notion of "governance based on virtue" and the spirit of "civilization."

CITATIONS

The people are not confined by boundaries, the state is not secured by dangerous cliffs and streams, and the world is not overawed by sharp weapons. The one who has Dao enjoys abundant support while the one who has lost Dao finds little support. When lack of support reaches its extreme point, even a ruler's own relatives will rebel against him. When abundant support reaches its extreme point, the whole world will follow him. If one whom the whole world follows attacks one whose own relatives rebel against him, the result is clear. Therefore, a man of virtue either does not go to war, or if he does, he is certain to win victory. (*Mencius*)

Jie and Zhou lost all under heaven because they lost the people. They lost the people because they lost the people's hearts. There is a way to win all under heaven: if you win the people, you win all under heaven. There is a way to win the people: if you win their hearts, you win the people. There is a way to win their hearts: amass for them what they desire, do not impose on them what they detest, and it is as simple as that. (*Mencius*)

219

déxìngzhīzhī

德性之知

Knowledge from One's Moral Nature

The term refers to knowledge derived from the functioning of the mind, which, in contrast to "knowledge from one's senses," transcends knowledge obtained through the sensory organs. Zhang Zai was the first to differentiate between "knowledge from one's senses" and "knowledge from one's moral nature." Confucian scholars of the Song Dynasty felt that people gained knowledge about the world in which they lived in two ways. Knowledge obtained from seeing and hearing was "knowledge from one's senses," whereas knowledge obtained through moral cultivation of the mind was "knowledge from one's moral nature." "Knowledge from one's moral nature" was not reliant on the sensor y organs; it transcended "knowledge from one's senses" and was fundamental knowledge about the world in which one lived.

CITATION

Knowledge from one's senses comes from contact with external objects and is not knowledge from one's moral nature. Knowledge from one's moral nature does not come from sensory perceptions. (Zhang Zai: *Enlightenment Through Confucian Teachings*)

220

diǎnyǎ

典雅

Classical Elegance

This term refers to a type of writing that is classically elegant. Originally, it meant that a piece of writing should be modeled on ancient classics, express pure and noble ideas, and follow classical literary styles by using Confucian doctrines for aesthetic guidance. Later, the term shifted to emphasize elegant diction and style that were free from vulgarity and frivolity. Later still, it gradually incorporated Daoist aesthetic views, suggesting natural tranquility and spiritual transcendence. For example, in "Twenty-four Styles of Poetry," Sikong Tu described classical elegance as being "as quiet as falling flower petals and as modest as unassuming daisies," which is close to the simple, relaxed, and natural style advocated by Daoist scholars.

CITATIONS

Classical elegance is achieved by emulating the Confucian classics and following Confucian doctrines in literary creation. (Liu Xie: *The Literary Mind and the Carving of Dragons*)

Xu Gan wrote his 20-chapter book *Discourses That Hit the Mark*, establishing a distinctive theory of his own. The carefully-researched, well-elaborated and highly elegant writings deserve to be passed on to future generations. (Cao Pi: A Letter to Wu Zhi)

221

dǐng

鼎

Ding (Vessel)

Ding was a vessel to cook food and was also used as an important ritual object in ancient times. Legend has it that Emperor Yu of the Xia Dynasty had nine *dings* cast, symbolizing the nine regions in the country. *Ding* was regarded as embodying the legitimacy and authority of the throne during the three dynasties of Xia, Shang, and Zhou. *Ding* was mostly cast in bronze, usually with two ears and three or four legs. The three legs stood for the "three chief ministers" (the three most powerful official positions in ancient times in charge of national civil administration, the judiciary, and military affairs). The four legs stood for the four advisors to the emperor. After the Qin Dynasty, *ding* gradually lost its function as a symbol of royal authority, but the word *ding* was still used to refer to the royal throne, the monarchy, or state power. It was also given the meaning of "glory," "grandeur," and "dignity."

CITATIONS

The *ding* was a vessel symbolizing the highest authority in an ancestral temple. (*The History of the Han Dynasty*)

A minister who wanted to seize the throne was referred to as one who inquired about the *ding*. (Liu Zhiji: *All About Historiography*)

222

dòngjìng
动静

Movement and Stillness

The term refers to two fundamental states in the existence of things, namely, movement and stillness. These two kinds of states are antithetic, but they also rely on each other and change into each other. Ancient Chinese had different views about the constant or the intrinsic state of the existence of things. Confucian scholars believed that "movement" was the fundamental state of existence of things, and that all things under heaven and on earth were in perpetual change and motion. Daoist scholars held that concrete things in motion were originally still, and that they would eventually return to stillness. Buddhists maintained that things were inherently all still and that the movements and changes people saw were just illusionary.

CITATIONS

There is a fundamental rule governing the movement and stillness of things, which determines if a thing is firm or gentle. (*The Book of Changes*)

When things stop to move, there is stillness. Fundamental stillness does not correspond to movement in concrete things. (Wang Bi: *Annotations on Laozi*)

One should explore stillness in every movement. By doing so, he can see that beneath movement there lies constant stillness. (Seng Zhao: *Treatises of Seng Zhao*)

223

duō xíng bù yì bì zì bì
多行不义必自毙

He Who Repeatedly Commits Wrongdoing Will Come to No Good End.

A person who repeatedly acts immorally will only end up in total failure. *Buyi* (不义) is an act which violates the principles of *yi* (义 righteousness). Righteousness is the moral code broadly accepted by a society; it is synonymous with *yi* (宜 propriety), meaning the observance of what is fit and proper. The Chinese have championed righteousness since ancient times, believing that all acts, whether those of individuals or of a nation, should be based on righteousness. Anyone who breaks laws, harms the country or the people, or commits numerous acts of wrongdoing will come to no good end.

CITATION

He who repeatedly commits wrongdoing will come to no good end. You just wait and see! (*Zuo's Commentary on The Spring and Autumn Annals*)

224

fánrù

繁缛

Overly Elaborative

This term refers to a literary writing style that is ornate and flowery in diction and excessively detailed and exhaustive in description, in contrast to being "simple and concise." The tendency to write elaborately about an idea in ornate language first emerged in the Western Jin Dynasty, represented by the writings of Lu Ji. His works were rich in allusions and antitheses, meticulous in diction and description, and elaborate and ornate in style. At the same time, these writings suffered from a lack of clarity and novelty. During the Qi and Liang of the Southern Dynasties, this overly elaborative style was listed as one of the eight major literary styles in Liu Xie's *The Literary Mind and the Carving of Dragons*.

CITATIONS

An overly elaborative style is known for its profuse use of allusions and ornate language to generate literary effect, like a tree branching out and a river forking into multiple streams. (Liu Xie: *The Literary Mind and the Carving of Dragons*)

Sometimes, one can employ flowery language in writing that makes the idea and language of a work mutually reinforcing, creating a refreshing and appealing effect in a consistently colorful style. It can be dazzling and gorgeous like a piece of exquisitely adorned brocade, or sentimental and lingering like an intricate piece of plaintive string music. (Lu Ji: *The Art of Writing*)

225

fēnggǔ
风骨

Fenggu

This term refers to powerful expressiveness and artistic impact that come from a literary work's purity of thoughts and emotions, as well as from its meticulously crafted structure. Despite some difference in interpreting the term, people tend to agree that *fenggu* (风骨) can be understood as being lucid and fresh in language while sturdy in structure. *Feng* (风) means "style," which emphasizes that a literary work should be based on pure thoughts, vivid impressions, and rich emotions so as to produce an effect of powerful expressiveness. *Gu* (骨) means "bones" or proper structure, figuratively. It stresses the impact of structure and sentence order, requiring a piece of writing to be robust, vigorous, profound, and yet succinct. If a piece of work is wordy and overly rhetorical but weak in content, then it lacks the impact of a "proper structure," no matter how flowery its expressions are. If such writing is awkward in delivery and has no emotions and vitality, then it lacks expressiveness in "style." *Fenggu* does not preclude, but rather combines with linguistic elegance in order to create a piece of good work. Good command of *fenggu* depends on the personality and dispositions of the author. In *The Literary Mind and the Carving of Dragons,* Liu Xie devoted a chapter to the discussion of *fenggu,* which is the first essay on writing style in the history of classical Chinese literary criticism.

CITATIONS

A piece of writing must have its own structure, and its own *fenggu,* that is, expressiveness in style and sturdiness in structure. How can it ever be the same as the writings of other writers! (*The History of Northern Wei*)

The charm of *fenggu* in a literary work derives from deliberate and precise diction that is hard to alter, and from powerful and controlled sounds that do not sound awkward when read out. (Liu Xie: *The Literary Mind and the Carving of Dragons*)

Once a good and appropriate style is set to make the writing lucid and vigorous, it will produce the effect of being pure, clear and powerfully impressive, making the writing both remarkable and appealing. (Liu Xie: *The Literary Mind and the Carving of Dragons*)

226

fēngjiào

风教

Moral Cultivation

Originally, this term meant to educate and influence people. Later, it came to refer to the function of shaping customary social practices, namely, the educational role of literary and artistic works in changing social behaviors and popular culture. Originating from "Preface to *Mao's Version of The Book of Songs*," the term is one of the important concepts of the Confucian school on the function of the arts. It believes that poetry and music have a role to play in shaping people's mind, reflecting the notion that rulers can educate and influence the general public by imparting a particular ideology in a top-down fashion, thereby achieving the desired effect of cultivating the general culture. The influence of this concept is far-reaching; it has impacted much of artistic creation in China, all the way from the poetry and music of the pre-Qin period to literary and artistic works in the modern times. It not only reflects the Confucian view on moral education, but also imparts a sense of social responsibility on writers and artists. However, if an artistic work overemphasizes moral cultivation, it runs the risk of placing ideology before artistic form, thus compromising its aesthetic value. The right way is to embed teaching in entertainment and let a literary or artistic work exert its influence on social mentality in a subtle and imperceptible way.

CITATIONS

"Guan Ju," the first ballad in a collection from the fifteen states in *The Book of Songs*, marks the starting point where moral education was conscientiously pursued by way of allegory. Its purpose was to educate and influence the general public and ensure the proper behavior between spouses. Moral cultivation can be conducted both at the individual and national levels. It is a concept derived from remonstration, as indicated by the first Chinese character of the term *feng*, which means to persuade and influence people by way of remonstration. (Preface to *Mao's Version of The Book of Songs*)

I once said that those who truly understand the writings of Tao Yuanming would be able to resist the temptations of personal fame and gains, and overcome greedy or stingy inclinations. With such understanding, a corrupted person would seek to attain integrity, and a timid one to become self-reliant; people would not only practice benevolence, but also decline offers of any official positions and salaries... This is how moral cultivation can be promoted. (Xiao Tong: Preface to *Collection of Tao Yuanming's Works*)

227

fúróng-chūshuǐ
芙蓉出水

Lotus Rising Out of Water

The term of lotus rising out of water describes a scene of freshness, quiet refinement and natural beauty, in contrast to "gilded and colored" embellishments. During the Wei and Jin dynasties, people valued nature and favored this aesthetic view. In their artistic creations, they pursued the natural and fresh style like lotus rising out of water. They sought natural presentation of their ideas and were opposed to excessive ornamentation.

CITATIONS

Xie Lingyun's poems are natural and refreshing like lotus rising out of water, whereas Yan Yanzhi's poems are elegantly embellished, like gilding an object and adding colors to it. (Zhong Rong: The Critique of Poetry)

It is like a lotus rising out of clear water: natural and without embellishment. (Li Bai: To Wei Liangzai, the Governor of Jiangxia Written While Thinking of My Friends on My Way into Exile at Yelang Following the War)

228

gāngróu-xiāngjì

刚柔相济

Combine Toughness with Softness

Gang (刚) and *rou* (柔) are two mutually complementary measures. They refer to two opposite properties or qualities that objects and human beings possess. In the realm of governance, *gang* means being tough and stern, while *rou* means being soft and lenient, and the term means to combine tough management with gentle care. *Gang* and *rou* are considered to be a concrete manifestation of yin and yang. Their mutual opposition and accommodation are the causes of change. When formulating and implementing policies and decrees or managing a society or an enterprise, there must be a certain balance between *gang* and *rou*.

CITATIONS

Confucius said: "One must perform righteousness according to the rules of propriety and speak in humility." One should be soft and gentle without, while tough and firm within, and should combine toughness with softness, without trying to overpower the other side. This is the way to achieve success in doing everything. (Zheng Shanfu: Letter in Reply to Daofu)

All generals must combine toughness with softness, and should not act with personal prowess only. (Luo Guanzhong: *Romance of the Three Kingdoms*)

229

gē
歌

Song

Songs are a kind of short, rhyming composition. It is a form of artistic creation combining literature, music, and even dance which can be sung. The difference between songs and poems in ancient China is that the former could be made into music and sung, whereas the latter could not. In a broad sense, the term includes children's ballads and folk ballads. In a narrow sense, songs and ballads are different. Songs have a fixed melody and musical accompaniment, while ballads do not. Songs were created mostly by folk musicians, such as "A Slow Song" of the Han Dynasty and the folk song "Song of the Chile" during the Northern Dynasties. A small number of songs, however, were written by members of the literati, like "Ode to the Great Wind" by Liu Bang and "The Midnight Melody of the Land of Wu" by Li Bai. Songs are one of the early forms of ancient Chinese poetic art and were generally classified as *yuefu* (乐府) poetry in ancient China. In modern times, they are called poetic songs as a part of poetry.

CITATION

Words sung with the accompaniment of music are called songs, and mere singing and chanting are called ballads. (*Mao's Version of The Book of Songs*)

230

gégù-dǐngxīn

革故鼎新

Do Away with the Old and Set Up the New

Do away with the old and set up the new. *Ge* (革) and *ding* (鼎) are two trigrams in *The Book of Changes*. In *Commentary on The Book of Changes*, it is explained that the lower *ge* trigram symbolizes fire and the upper *ge* trigram symbolizes water. Since fire and water are opposed and in conflict, and they cannot keep an original state of equilibrium, changes are bound to occur. Consequently, the *ge* trigram implies change of an unsuitable old state of affairs. The lower *ding* trigram symbolizes wood and the upper *ding* trigram symbolizes fire. When people throw the wood into the fire, they can cook their food in a *ding*. Thus, the *ding* trigram signifies the creation of new things. Following the doctrine in *Commentary on The Book of Changes*, later people combined the two together to represent an outlook advocating changes.

CITATION

Ge trigram signifies doing away with the old; *ding* trigram symbolizes setting up the new. (*The Book of Changes*)

231

gōng shēng míng, lián shēng wēi
公生明，廉生威

Fairness Fosters Discernment and Integrity Creates Authority.

Only by being fair can one distinguish between right and wrong; only with moral conduct can one establish authority. These mottoes were used as reminders by upright officials of the Ming and Qing dynasties. *Gong* (公) means fairness and opposing pursuit of selfish interest. *Ming* (明) means discernment, namely, the ability to distinguish right from wrong. *Lian* (廉) means free from corruption. *Wei* (威) means authority or credibility. Today, these teachings have remained important principles which office holders should abide by. They mean that governance should be exercised in a fair and just way and within the framework of laws and regulatory procedures of the state. Officials should lead by example, have moral integrity and be self-disciplined; they should put public interests above their own and not use their power to pursue personal gain.

CITATION

Officials have a sense of awe towards me not because of my being strict with them, but because of my upright conduct. People accept my authority not because of my ability, but because of my fairness. If I am fair, people will not dare to disobey my order; if I am morally upright, officials will not dare to deceive me. Only by being fair can one distinguish between right and wrong; only with moral integrity can one establish authority. (Nian Fu: Mottoes for Officials, from a stone carving)

232

hàoránzhīqì

浩然之气

Noble Spirit

Noble spirit is a powerful source of cultivating integrity in one's life. In Mencius' view, it goes hand in hand with morality and justice and originates from within rather than from without. If one lives an ethical life and regularly conducts soul searching, he will be imbued with noble spirit and will willingly stand up for what is right.

CITATION

"May I ask what noble spirit is?" "It is something hard to describe," Mencius answered. "As a vital force, it is immensely powerful and just. Cultivate it with rectitude and keep it unharmed, and it will fill all the space between heaven and earth. Being a vital force, noble spirit becomes powerful with the accompaniment of righteousness and Dao. Without righteousness and Dao, noble spirit will be weak and frail." (*Mencius*)

233

jìtuō

寄托

Entrusting

The term refers to the entrusting of the poet's subjective understanding or sentiments to imagery in poetic works. It can also stir responsive appreciation of the reader. *Ji* (寄) means having a specific thought or individual feelings, and *tuo* (托) means giving expression to such thought or feelings through the channel of an object. It is a literary term first used by a group of *ci* (词 lyric) poets from Changzhou during the Qing Dynasty. Zhang Huiyan stressed that lyric writing should follow the tradition of analogies, associations and allegories in *The Book of Songs*. Zhou Ji further suggested that an aspiring poet should entrust his thought to imagery in order to raise the artistic appeal of his work and stimulate the imagination of the reader. After having established himself, however, the poet should not be bound by the technique of entrusting to imagery; rather, his words and sentiments should blend seamlessly. This view emphasized the primacy of nature of literature as opposed to the primacy of concept and provided a new guidance for literary creation at the time.

CITATION

When writing *ci* poetry, one cannot effectively express one's thoughts and sentiments without entrusting them to imagery. On the other hand, overreliance on imagery will make it hard for one to clearly express his idea. (Zhou Ji: Preface to *Contents of Selected Poems of the Four Poets of the Song Dynasty*)

234

jiànlì-sīyì

见利思义

Think of Righteousness in the Face of Gain

When faced with gain one should first consider and distinguish whether the obtainment of gain is in accord with morality. This is a Confucian criterion for dealing with the relation between righteousness and gain. Between the pursuit of gain and the upholding of morality a conflict has long existed. Because people more often than not may covet personal gain and overlook morality, their actions may go against virtue and violate the law. Against this kind of situation Confucius advanced the stand of "thinking of righteousness in the face of gain," proposing that people should strive for gain on the basis of the principle of morality. He who knows morality is a man of virtue, and he who blindly pursues gain is a petty man.

CITATION

He who when faced with gain thinks of righteousness, who when confronted with danger is ready to lay down his life, and who does not forget a past promise despite enduring poverty, may be considered a true man! (*The Analects*)

235

jiànwénzhīzhī

见闻之知

Knowledge from One's Senses

The term refers to knowledge derived from contact between externalities and one's sensory organs such as the ears and eyes, in contrast to "knowledge from one's moral nature." Zhang Zai was the first to differentiate between "knowledge from one's senses" and "knowledge from one's moral nature." Confucian scholars of the Song Dynasty felt that people acquired knowledge about the world in which they lived in two ways. Knowledge obtained from seeing and hearing was "knowledge from the senses," which was an essential part of human knowledge. However, it was not a complete picture, nor could it provide an understanding of the original source or ontological existence of the world.

CITATION

Knowledge from one's senses is not knowledge from one's moral nature. It comes from contact with external objects and not from the inner workings of the heart. (*Writings of the Cheng Brothers*)

236

jiànxián-sīqí

见贤思齐

When Seeing a Person of High Caliber, Strive to Be His Equal.

This term means that when you see a person of high caliber, you should try to emulate and equal the person. *Xian* (贤) refers to a person of virtue and capability; *qi* (齐) means to emulate and reach the same level. This was what Confucius taught his students to do. The term has become a motto for cultivating one's moral character and increasing one's knowledge. The main point of this term is to encourage people to discover the strengths of others and take initiative to learn from those who are stronger than themselves in terms of moral qualities, knowledge, and skills so as to make constant progress. The term embodies the Chinese nation's spirit for good, enterprise, and tenacious self-renewal.

CITATIONS

Confucius said, "When you see a person of virtue and capability, you should think of emulating and equaling the person; when you see a person of low caliber, you should reflect on your own weak points." (*The Analects*)

Men of virtue, who study extensively and reflect on themselves every day, become wise and intelligent and are free from making mistakes. (*Xunzi*)

237

jiàngǔ-zhījīn
鉴古知今

Review the Past to Understand the Present

Reviewing the past helps us understand the present and predict the future. It is also said that "reviewing the past we understand the future" and "knowing the past we understand the present." The Chinese word *jian* (鉴) can mean "mirror" and hence to "review the past" as if in a mirror, "understand the past," or "gain knowledge of the past." The lessons of the rise and fall of dynasties and states, the words and deeds of historical figures, as well as right and wrong, and good and evil, help govern the country and improve personal morality. "Understanding the present," "reviewing the present," or "understanding the future" means predicting the future based on the present. The rulers of antiquity saw it as extremely important to draw lessons from history in order to avoid past mistakes and justify their policies by making them conform to the needs of the country and people. The concept of "reviewing the past to understand the present" stresses both the practical significance of history and the historical depth of things present. It is similar to the concept that "past experience, if not forgotten, is a guide for the future."

CITATIONS

It is advisable to review the rise and fall of previous dynasties and the achievements and failures of the present dynasty, to commend the good, condemn the evil, and adopt what is right and discard what is wrong. (Sima Guang: Memorial on *History as a Mirror*)

It is of great importance to review knowledge of the past to help understand the present, expel the invasion of the State of Wei and wipe out the State of Wu. (*A Peace Banquet*)

238

jìnxīn

尽心

Exert One's Heart / Mind to the Utmost

"Exerting one's mind to the utmost" means one should fully understand and extend one's innate goodness. It is a way of moral cultivation advocated by Mencius. To do so, one needs to develop one's capability of thinking, discover the goodness inherent in the mind and then fully nurture this innate human character, eventually realizing the moral qualities of benevolence, righteousness, rites and social norms, and wisdom.

CITATIONS

Mencius said, "He who does his utmost knows his nature. Knowing his nature, he knows his inborn moral nature. Preserving his mind and nurturing his nature is the way to deal with his inherent morality. (*Mencius*)

Exerting one's mind to the utmost means knowing the laws of all things, with nothing left out. (*Classified Conversations of Master Zhu Xi*)

239

kōnglíng

空灵

Ethereal Effect

This refers to an open, free, and flexible style of a work of art; it is the opposite of a "densely packed" work of art. Ethereal effect does not mean sheer emptiness; it does not completely avoid imagery, nor does it entirely avoid natural description. Rather its aim is to suggest unlimited possibilities for the viewer's imagination through a highly economical use of brushwork and imagery so as to pursue the "meaning that lies beyond literal form" or "associations beyond the work itself." In this way it leaves room for the viewer's imagination. For example, just as redundant description is deliberately left out of an essay or a poem, along with ponderous wording or unnecessary images, just so thick ink and heavy colors may be avoided in painting. The notion of ethereal effect values simple layout and an economical use of details, seeking to convey character and imagination. Works that make use of ethereal effect convey a wonderful lucidity, and possess openness, freedom, and natural grace. Such works enable viewers to appreciate the aesthetic joy of free imagination.

CITATIONS

When painting, classical artists made use of ethereal effect all the more where a dense collection of objects normally was required. However today's artists no sooner begin to paint than they fill the space with elaborate details. In fact, if a painter applies a few specific details strategically in the empty spaces, then the whole picture will appear more open and alive. Under the circumstances the more images he uses, the less boring the picture. (Yun Shouping: *Nantian's Comments on Paintings*)

Some essays are written in a substantive style, whereas others feature an ethereal style. Although these two kinds of writing have their respective merits, they are each lopsided in their own way. But if one reads Han Yu's essays, he will find that they are a perfect combination of substantive content and ethereal effect. (Liu Xizai: *Overview of Literary Theories*)

240

kuàngdá
旷达

Broad-mindedness / Unconstrained Style

The term means broad-mindedness and a totally unconstrained artistic style in poetic works. It presents a perfect union of the author's outlook on life, his peaceful mind, and the artistic form of his work. A broad-minded writer was often disheartened, who went into seclusion, caused either by frustrations countered in life or social turmoil, and he would naturally seek to express his emotion in literature. As reflected in his writings, such a writer possessed a keen insight into the vicissitudes of worldly affairs. Being cynical and indignant, he also revealed such feelings of disdain for the world and its ways in his writings. The origin of this attitude can be traced back to the Confucian concept of proactivity and the Daoist proposition of following the nature, as well as to the open and cultured way of life characteristic of famous scholars of the Wei and Jin dynasties. Such a writer would not shy away from the worldly, but neither would he cling to fame and wealth. He was completely reasonable in attitude and tolerant in mood. Sikong Tu, a literary critic in the Tang Dynasty, used this term to assess poetic and aesthetic achievement by emphasizing the unity of the style of a work and the mental attitude and the view about human life on the part of the author. The idea is to promote a view about life and an aesthetic attitude that is open-minded and uplifting.

CITATION

There are no more than a hundred years in a man's life, so what difference does it make whether it is long or short! Joys are painfully brief, but sorrows are numerous. There is nothing like holding a goblet of drink, strolling in the mist and the quiet and shady garden, or watching rain drizzling down the thatched eaves covered with flowers! After finishing the drink, I will just take another stroll and sing! Who can escape from one's last day? Only the Zhongnan Mountains will forever stay lofty. (Sikong Tu: Twenty-four Styles of Poetry)

241

lǐshàngwǎnglái

礼尚往来

Reciprocity as a Social Norm

Etiquette requires reciprocity and mutual benefit. It refers to contacts and interactions between individuals, between organizations, and between nations and implies equality and mutual benefit in interpersonal and inter-state relations. Sometimes, it also means that one should treat the other party in the way the other party treats you. It is similar to "Treating the other person the way he treats you."

CITATION

Etiquette values reciprocity and mutual benefit. It would go against it if someone who has received a gift does not reciprocate such goodwill. When one acts according to such etiquette, one will enjoy peace. Without it, one will cause trouble. (*The Book of Rites*)

242

lǐyī-fēnshū

理一分殊

There Is But One *Li* (Universal Principle), Which Exists in Diverse Forms.

Being a supreme domain in terms of principle, *li* (理) exists in different things and manifests itself in different forms. "There is but one *li*, which exists in diverse forms" – this is an important way in which the Song- and Ming-dynasty thinkers viewed the forms in which *li* exists. As *li* has different meanings, its one-and-diverse composition is also interpreted in different ways. First, as the origin of universe in an ontological sense, *li* runs through all things. The *li* of each thing is not a part of *li*, rather, it is endowed with the full meaning of *li*. Second, representing the universal law governing all things, the universal *li* expresses itself in the form of different guiding principles in specific things. The *li* of each thing or being is a concrete expression of the universal *li*. The concept of *li* being one and same ensures unity of the world, whereas its diversity provides the basis for multifarious things and hierarchical order.

CITATIONS

Li (universal principle) runs through all things, which is derived from one source. But as *li* is present in different things, its functions and forms vary. (*Classified Conversations of Master Zhu Xi*)

When a person or thing comes into being and is endowed with *qi*, or vital force, he or it is governed by only one *li* (universal principle). However, once a person or thing gains a specific physical form, the *li* embodied expresses itself in different ways. (Luo Qinshun: *Knowledge Painfully Acquired*)

243

nèiměi

内美

Inner Beauty

Inner beauty means a fine disposition and moral character. It first appeared in Li Sao by Qu Yuan, referring to an inherited innate moral character which was further fostered in one's early living environment. On this basis acquired competence develops, which is achieved when one, after gaining initial understanding of the principles of things, consciously improves his moral character through self-cultivation, and strengthens one's abilities. Later this term is used to emphasize that an author should possess an inner fine disposition and moral character, and that noble and great literature can only derive from a noble and great character.

CITATIONS

Armed with such moral qualities given me by birth, I continue to develop competence. (Qu Yuan: *Li Sao*)

In literary creation, one must have both moral standard and outstanding capabilities. Neither is dispensable. As *ci* lyrics give expression to emotions, one must focus on bringing out the inner beauty. (Wang Guowei: *Poetic Remarks in the Human World – An Edition with Deletions*)

244

pǐjí-tàilái
否极泰来

When Worse Comes to the Worst, Things Will Turn for the Better.

When worse comes to the worst, things and events at their extremes will reverse and turn for the better. *Tai* (泰) and *pi* (否), two of the hexagram names in *The Book of Changes*, represent the positive and negative aspects of things, with one unimpeded and the other blocked, one faced with favorable conditions and the other with adversity, and one good and the other bad. In the view of ancient Chinese, all things cycle around and forever change. When they reach a certain critical point, they will transform into the opposite of their extreme characteristics. The term reveals the dialectical movements of development and change. It gives moral support and hope to people experiencing difficulties, and encourages people to be optimistic, seize the opportunity, work hard, and turn things around. From a dialectical perspective, it represents a sense of preparing for the worst.

CITATION

The picture of heaven above and earth down is *tai* hexagram while that of the other way round is *pi* hexagram. *Tai* means things are smooth and unimpeded, while *pi* means things are blocked. Likewise, *tai* means "open" while *pi* means "closed." With one unimpeded and the other blocked, one open and the other closed, the two form a circle. It is a common phenomenon to replace each other regularly, like winter and summer, and day and night, moving on in cycles. Even heaven and earth, as well as sages, cannot escape from changing. (Lin Li: *Notes and Commentaries on The Book of Changes*)

245

piāoyì
飘逸

Natural Grace

Natural grace, a term for poetic study (often in contrast to the "melancholy" poetic style), refers to free and unconstrained aesthetic style and artistic appeal in poetic works. It gives expression to the imagination of the poet, the natural and free disposition of his spirit, and his pursuit of aesthetic enjoyment. When in such a state of mind, the poet is "totally absorbed in his interaction with heaven and earth," roaming freely in boundless time and space. The concept represents a poetic style in which the poet and what he portrays in his poem merge into a natural whole.

CITATION

Du Fu could not write as freely and unconstrained as Li Bai, while the latter did not possess the style of melancholy and profoundness typical of Du Fu's poems. (Yan Yu: *Canglang's Criticism of Poetry*)

246

qíwù

齐物

Seeing Things as Equal

This refers to a worldview or lifestyle that seeks to reconcile differences and contradictions among things. In "On Seeing things as equal", Zhuangzi analyzes the unpredictable nature of the world to reveal that different or opposing things are inherently interconnected. In striving to understand the world, one should therefore first of all identify the interconnectedness among all things in the world, see all as equal, and abandon personal preferences, likes and dislikes. In this way, one's heart can be above all material things and free from their constraints and influences, and the differences and contradictions among things will no longer burden one's mind or one's life.

CITATION

Hence if we can see all things as equal, there will be no flaws brought about by our personal preferences. (Guo Xiang: *Annotations on Zhuangzi*)

247

qì
器

Qi (Vessel)

Qi (器) is a real object or a specific official, position, etc. A *qi* is something visible, or something one may describe in concrete terms. Every kind of *qi* has a specific form, function, or capability. Therefore there are clear distinctions between one *qi* and another. However, a common Dao exists in different *qis*. The existence of a *qi* is based on Dao. In terms of human affairs, an individual assumes a particular responsibility suited to his position; but he should go beyond his specific capabilities and strive to adhere to and obtain Dao.

CITATIONS

What is above form is called Dao, and what is under form is called "an object." (*The Book of Changes*)

Confucius said, "A virtuous man should not possess one skill only." (*The Analects*)

Dao disperses and gives birth to tangible objects, and sages who are good at making use of objects of different functions become natural leaders of all officials. (*Laozi*)

248

qìgǔ

气骨

Qigu (Emotional Vitality and Forcefulness)

This term refers to the emotional strength and the vitality of a literary work. It was first used during the Southern Dynasties, resonating with the social practice of making comment on people. The term was used to describe the emotional vigor and forcefulness of artistic works such as poetry, essays, calligraphy, and paintings. It is similar in meaning to *fenggu* (风骨), but contrary to *fengzi* (风姿), a term meaning external elegance of an artistic work.

CITATIONS

In terms of its emotional vitality and forcefulness, the poem stands equal to works of the Jian'an Reign period; in terms of its musicality and rhythms, it surpasses the works of the Taikang Reign period. (Yin Fan: *A Collection of Poems by Distinguished Poets*)

This piece of calligraphy by Lord Lu (Yan Zhenqing) is amazing, vigorous, mellow, and forceful, fully illustrating the admirable emotional vitality and strength that characterized the style since the Wei, Jin, Sui and Tang dynasties. (Huang Tingjian: Inscription on Lord Lu's Calligraphy)

249

qìzhìzhīxìng

气质之性

Character Endowed by *Qi* (Vital Force)

The moral characters of humans endowed or influenced by *qi* (气) stand in contrast with "heavenly endowed characters" or the "properties of heaven and ear th." The term encompasses two meanings. First, it refers to the specific disposition of a person under the influence of *qi*, such as firmness and gentleness, patience and impatience, and wisdom and stupidity. Biased and unkind behaviors of people originate from the "properties of *qi*." In this sense, the "properties of *qi*" and the "properties of heaven and earth" together constitute a person's inborn character. Second, it means that heavenly laws and *qi* together influence a person's character. As heavenly laws are imbedded in the physical human body, they are influenced by *qi*. The interaction of moral characters endowed by heavenly laws and human desires reflects the properties of *qi* (vital force).

CITATIONS

Physical matters take up their shape which acquires the nature of *qi* (vital force); if we are thus good at returning to it, then the nature endowed by heaven and earth will be preserved. (Zhang Zai: *Enlightenment Through Confucian Teachings*)

As for the properties of heaven and earth, they refer exclusively to heavenly laws. As for the nature of *qi*, it refers to the combination of heavenly laws and *qi*. (*Classified Conversations of Master Zhu Xi*)

250

qiánshì-bùwàng, hòushìzhīshī
前事不忘，后事之师

Past Experience, If Not Forgotten, Is a Guide for the Future.

This concept is meant to remind people of the need to learn from past experience and make it a guide for the future. In ancient China great importance was attached to writing history and thus historiography experienced great progress. It was so designed as to review the successes and failures of previous dynasties and recount the good and evil in historical figures, especially sovereigns and officials, in order to provide a warning or a guide for the future.

CITATIONS

In observing past events and learning of ancient times, I have found that the good things in the world are always the same, but it has never occurred that when a sovereign and his officials have had equal power, they can still live harmoniously. We should not forget past experience, but instead use it as a guide for the future. (*Strategies of the Warring States*)

I have heard that past events are a guide to future events and that the words and actions of ancient people provide models for people of the present age. Even though time has changed, they are not off the mark in providing criteria for right and wrong. (Zhao Pu: Memorial Urging Emperor Taizong to Withdraw Troops)

251

qiú fàngxīn

求放心

Search for the Lost Heart

To search for and retrieve one's lost heart is a way to cultivate one's morality propounded by Mencius. In his view everyone was born with a benevolent heart, which meant the "four beginnings" of benevolence, righteousness, rites and social norms, and wisdom. These are virtues conferred by Heaven and the sources of human kindness. However, people may be influenced by external factors or the environment when growing up. In that case, their innate goodness may be weakened or obscured and hence they may act or speak in contrary to moral principles. Therefore, when cultivating one's moral character, one must find and recover one's innate good heart.

CITATION

One surely knows to look for the chicken or dog and bring them back when he loses them. However, one may not know to look for his heart when he loses it. The way of learning is no other than searching for one's lost heart. (*Mencius*)

252

qǔ
曲

Qu (Melody)

Qu (曲) is a literary form that came into being later than poetry and *ci* (词). It generally refers to the northern- and southern-style melodies created in the Song and Jin dynasties. Northern melodies were composed mostly with tunes in northern China and performed in northern dialect, while southern melodies had southern tunes and southern dialect. Since *qu* reached its peak in the Yuan Dynasty, it is generally known as Yuan *qu* or Yuan opera. *Qu* is similar to *ci* in form but is more flexible in sentence structure, and colloquial language is used. There are two main types of *qu*: one is northern *zaju* (杂剧) opera and southern *chuanqi* (传奇) opera; such *qu* is known as *xiqu* (戏曲) or *juqu* (剧曲). The other type is *sanqu* (散曲) or lyric songs, also known as *qingqu* (清曲). As with other forms of poetry, *sanqu* describes a scene, a sentiment or an event and can be sung, but it has no spoken parts or instructions for performers' movements and expressions. Generally speaking, the old-style opera is much more accomplished and influential than *sanqu*. The Yuan period was a golden age in the development of Chinese opera. There are more than 80 known playwrights from that time. Guan Hanqing, Bai Pu, Ma Zhiyuan, and Zheng Guangzu represent different styles from different stages of the Yuan opera, and they are recognized as the four leading Yuan opera writers. Yuan opera has distinctive plots and artistic appeal. Together with Tang and Song poetry and Ming and Qing fiction, it marks an important milestone in the historical development of Chinese literature.

CITATION

When it comes to leading opera writers of the Yuan Dynasty, Guan Hanqing, Zheng Guangzu, Bai Pu, and Ma Zhiyuan come to mind. (Wang Jide: *On the Melody and Writing of Chinese Operas*)

253

rénzhě'àirén

仁者爱人

The Benevolent Person Loves Others.

The benevolent person has a loving heart. *Renzhe* (仁者) refers to benevolent and virtuous people or people with loving hearts, who have tremendous courage, wisdom, perfect moral character, charm, and charisma, and who love and care about others. Confucianism holds *ren* (仁) as the highest moral value. The basic meaning of *ren* is loving others, and to love others, one should first show filial piety to one's parents and respect one's elder brothers, and then extend love and care to other family members, and eventually to everyone else in the world. Mencius synthesized and upgraded this notion into a theory to be applied to the governance of a country. He proposed that a person of virtue should love and care about first his loved ones, then other people, and finally everything on earth. Confucianism believed that love could be extended to people in a certain order, but that benevolence has universal value, which is both the foundation and the goal of building a harmonious and good-will society.

CITATIONS

He who is benevolent loves others, and he who having manners respects others. He who loves others is loved by others and he who respects others is respected by others. (*Mencius*)

Men of virtue love and care for their loved ones, they are therefore kind to other people. When they are kind to people, they treasure everything on earth. (*Mencius*)

254

sānbiǎo

三表

Three Standards

The term means the three standards used to measure the truth of an assertion. The Chinese character *biao* (表) in this term means standard or norm. Mozi believed in judging right or wrong by following the three standards. The first one was the successful way in which the ancient sage kings had ruled. The second one was the actual experience of the people. The third one was whether one's words and deeds actually served the interests of the state and people. Mozi established his school of thought on the basis of the three standards and used them to evaluate and criticize the doctrines of other schools.

CITATION

To make assertions one must establish a standard of judgment. Speaking without a standard is analogous to trying to determine the time of sunrise and sunset on a revolving potter's wheel. Distinctions of right and wrong, benefit and harm, cannot be clearly derived. Therefore, we must have the three standards. (*Mozi*)

255

sāncái

三才

The Three Elements

The Three Elements refer to heaven, earth, and man. When explaining the trigrams, *Commentary on The Book of Changes* proposes the idea of "the Three Elements." In a trigram which consists of six undivided and divided lines, the first and second lines at the bottom represent earth, the third and fourth lines in the center represent man who lives between earth and heaven, and the fifth and sixth lines at the upper part represent heaven. Collectively, the six lines united in one diagram signify the whole of heaven, earth, and man. The three elements share the same rules but have different manifestations of rules in their each field.

CITATIONS

So the law of heaven is governed by yin and yang; the law of earth is governed by softness and hardness; and the law of man is governed by benevolence and righteousness. Each trigram, described in *The Book of Changes*, consists of six lines with each two being a unit representing heaven, earth and man. (*The Book of Changes*)

Each trigram in *The Book of Changes* consists of three elements: the *qi* of yin and yang representing heaven, the quality of softness and hardness representing earth, and the virtue of benevolence and righteousness representing man. (Zhang Zai: *Zhang Zai's Explanation of The Book of Changes*)

256

sānsī'érxíng

三思而行

Think Thrice Before Acting

Originally the term referred to taking action only after having reflected thrice. This is a kind of attitude handling things too cautiously. An appropriate measure of reflection is a prerequisite for proper speech and action, but if one becomes too cautious, then hesitation and doubt easily arise in the mind, affecting the observance of morality in the face of personal gain. *The Analects* records that Ji Wenzi, a senior official of the State of Lu, "acted having reflected thrice." Confucius thought that it would suffice if Ji reflected twice and that there was no need to reflect three times. When people later used the expression "thinking thrice before acting," they weakened the meaning of being too cautious, and just used it to urge caution when acting. They stressed that one should carefully reflect before speaking or acting so as to be in conformity with accepted moral standards.

CITATION

Ji Wenzi acted after having reflected thrice. When Confucius heard it, he remarked, "Twice is sufficient." (*The Analects*)

257

shèndú
慎独

Shendu

A kind of ethical self-cultivation advanced by the Confucian school of thought, the term has two different meanings: First, *du* (独) is understood as at leisure and alone. When people are alone, without someone else's supervision, they easily act in an undisciplined and immoral way. *Shendu* (慎独) requires being careful with one's conduct when being alone, consciously following morality and the requirements of etiquette. Second, *du* is understood as an inner true state. People may in their words and actions manifest what is in accord with morality and the requirements of etiquette, but in their heart they do not accept or pursue any morality or etiquette. *Shendu* requires that one makes efforts in one's heart, so that one's inner world is in agreement with the words and actions required by morality and etiquette.

CITATIONS

A man of virtue is cautious when he is not being watched by others and apprehensive when what he says is not being heard. There is nothing more visible than in what is secret, and nothing more obvious than in what is vague and minute. Therefore, a man of virtue is watchful when he is at leisure and alone. (*The Book of Rites*)

This means what one truly believes in his heart and mind will find expression in the open. That is why a man of virtue must be cautious when he is at leisure and alone. (*The Book of Rites*)

258

shènsī-míngbiàn

慎思明辨

Careful Reflection and Clear Discrimination

It was thought in ancient China that a person matured through five stages: broad study for collecting information and acquiring knowledge, close examination for identifying problems and resolving doubts, careful reflection for absorbing and mastering knowledge, clear discrimination for developing concepts and reaching conclusions, and earnest practice for putting knowledge into practice and developing character. These stages can be roughly divided into three areas: learning, reflection, and practice. "Careful reflection and clear discrimination" describes the stage of reflection between learning and practice. It can also be said that study and reflection on the one hand and study and practice on the other complement each other, while reflection is a deepening and heightening of learning, a prerequisite for practice, and a key link between learning and practice.

CITATION

Learn broadly, examine closely, reflect carefully, discriminate clearly, and practice earnestly. (*The Book of Rites*)

259

shī

诗

Shi (Poetry)

Shi (诗) is a major genre of ancient Chinese literature, the earliest literary form that emerged in China. Observing the requirements of a certain rhythm, rules of rhyming, number of characters, and type of verses, and using concise language and rich imagination, it reflects social life and conveys thoughts and emotions. *Shi* and *wen* (文) are two principal forms of ancient Chinese literature. *Shi*, as referred to by the ancient Chinese, consists of the older type of poetry and the latter type of poetry. It generally does not include *ci* (词 lyric) and *qu* (曲 melody), which appeared as literary genres after the Tang Dynasty. The older type of *shi* is also called *gufeng* (古风), meaning ancient style, which is a general appellation for all kinds of poetic forms produced prior to the latter type of *shi*, except the style employed in the odes of Chu. With relatively few restrictions in rules and forms, *shi* is not constrained by any antithetical arrangement or a fixed tone pattern, and its rhyme is fairly free. In addition, the length of a piece is not limited. A verse may have four, six, seven, or a mixed number of Chinese characters. The latter type of *shi* is also called *gelüshi* (格律诗), meaning poetry with fixed patterns. Its number of characters, rhyming, tone pattern, and antithetical arrangement are all strictly fixed. A poem of this type may contain four lines (known as *jue* 绝), each with five or seven characters, or eight lines (known as *lü* 律), each with five or seven characters. Occasionally, it is much longer than normal, expanding to one and a half dozen lines, which is referred to as *pailü* (排律). The difference between *shi*, and *ci* and *qu* is that the former is not set to music, while the latter may be set to music and sung. *Shi* has existed as a literary form for more than 2,000 years in China. Ancient Chinese used *shi* to connect humans with nature, voice aspirations, and give expression to emotions. It embodied the spirit and aesthetic pursuits of literature and art in ancient China, which is very different from the West, which only sees poetry as a category of literature. In ancient China, Confucian thought played an important guiding role in poetic creation, while Daoist and Buddhist thoughts had a profound influence on the theory of poetry's artistic conception. Since *The Book of Songs* was China's earliest collection of poems, later generations also used *shi* to refer to *The Book of Songs* in particular.

CITATIONS

Shi gives expression to aspirations while songs are verses for chanting. In singing, *shi* undergoes changes in tempo and tone; then it harmonizes sounds with meter and melody. (*The Book of History*)

Shi expresses aspirations through written words, whereas songs do so via chanting. Dancing is a sequence of body movements to project one's emotions. All these three forms of art come forth from the heart, accompanied by musical performance. (*The Book of Rites*)

The four seasons bring changes in scenery, which in turn stir one's emotions. One gives expression to such emotions through dancing and chanting. Poetry thus illuminates heaven, earth and humans, making everything clear and bright. The gods in heaven rely on it to perform sacrificial rituals and the spirits in the nether world use it to communicate with the world. Among those which move heaven, earth and the spirits, nothing comes near poetry! (Zhong Rong: Preface to"The Critique of Poetry")

260

shīzhí-wéizhuàng
师直为壮

Troops Will Be Powerful When Fighting a Just Cause.

This term suggests that when there is a good cause to use military force, the troops will be high in morale and valiant in fighting. The word *shi* (师) here is a general term for all military forces and operations. The word *zhi* (直) means a just cause. The word *zhuang* (壮) means powerful troops. The Chinese nation has always been wary of waging wars, believing that a war should be fought only for a just cause and that an army fighting for such a cause will have high morale and wins the war.

CITATION

In fighting a just war, the troops will have high morale and be powerful, while they suffer from poor morale when the cause is unjust. Morale has nothing to do with how long an army is deployed at the front. (*Zuo's Commentary on The Spring and Autumn Annals*)

261

shòurényǐyú

授人以渔

Teaching How to Fish

This term expresses the idea that giving away a fish is not as good as teaching one how to fish. The meaning is that rather than giving something away it is better to teach the method of obtaining it so that people can get what they need through their own efforts. It implies that once an objective is established, the method of achieving it becomes most important, and that the effective way of helping and managing people in the long term is to encourage them to be self-supporting.

CITATION

To give people a fish and you only provide them with one meal; to teach them to fish and they can benefit throughout their lives. (Chinese proverb)

262

shù

恕

Being Considerate / Forgiveness

The basic meaning of the term is to put oneself in another person's position and have empathy, and to reflect what one would do in the same kind of situation. Starting out from their own likes and dislikes, people can understand and show considerations for the wishes of others, and on the basis of such understanding, people should refrain from imposing their own likes and dislikes on others. This is what it means to be considerate. To those enforcing the law and to the victims of wrongdoing, the meaning of the term extended to mean forgiveness or pardon.

CITATIONS

Zigong asked, "Is there any teaching that can serve as a lasting principle for conduct in one's whole life?" Confucius replied, "Surely that is to be considerate! Do not do to others what you do not want others to do to you." (*The Analects*)

To extend one's mind to understand others is called "being considerate". (Zhu Xi: *The Analects Variorum*)

263

sì hǎi zhī nèi jiē xiōng dì

四海之内皆兄弟

All the People Within the Four Seas Are Brothers.

This saying means that all the people in the world are as close as brothers. The Four Seas are the East, West, South, and North seas. The ancient Chinese believed that heaven was round and the earth was square, with China in the middle of the earth, which was surrounded on all four sides by the Four Seas. "Within the Four Seas" refers to the world inhabited by humans, which was also called "all under heaven," referring to the whole country or the whole world. This saying shows the inclusive and broad mind of the Chinese and their compassion, love and friendship towards other human beings.

CITATION

Zixia said, "So long as a man of virtue always does things conscientiously without making mistakes and treats people respectfully and appropriately, then all the people within the Four Seas will be his brothers. Why should he then worry about having no brothers?" (*The Analects*)

264

tàixū

太虚

Taixu (Great Void)

Taixu (太虚) refers to a state of void in both space and things. Zhang Zai, a thinker in the Song Dynasty, elaborated on the meaning of *taixu*, or great void. He believed that all things in heaven and on earth were made up of *qi* (气), and that *taixu* was its natural state, which was formless and motionless. When *taixu* coalesced, it turned into *qi*; when *qi* dissipated, it became *taixu*. Though *taixu* could not be felt by humans, it was not absolute emptiness and nothingness. *Taixu* gave life to all things in heaven and on earth by means of *qi*.

CITATIONS

And so, they will not be able to go beyond Mount Kunlun, nor can they wander in the great void. (*Zhuangzi*)

Taixu is formless; it is the original state of *qi*. Whether *qi* coalesces or dissipates, it is just a temporary form of *taixu*, or great void. (Zhang Zai: *Enlightenment Through Confucian Teachings*)

265

tiāndào

天道

Way of Heaven

The way of heaven refers to the basic rule governing the existence and changes of all things between heaven and earth, as opposed to "the way of humans." Ancient Chinese interpreted "the way of heaven" in different ways. First, some believed that "the way of heaven," especially the celestial phenomena relating to the movements of the sun, the moon, and the stars, foretell or dictate the success or failure of human affairs. In ancient times, designated officials predicted human affairs through observing celestial phenomena. Second, some believed that "the way of heaven" was the source or the basis of man's moral conduct and of orderly human relations. One should comply with "the way of heaven," in both words and deeds, so should human relations; and people should recognize and develop the moral nature bestowed upon by heaven so as to gain access to "the way of heaven." Third, still others thought that there were no particular correlations between "the way of heaven" on the one hand, and moral conduct in the human world, human relations, as well as misfortune and fortune in human affairs on the other.

CITATIONS

The laws governing the ways of heaven are yin and yang, those governing the ways of earth are gentleness and firmness, and those governing the ways of human society are benevolence and righteousness. (*The Book of Changes*)

Integrity is what the way of nature requires; acting with integrity is the way to achieve self-refinement. (*The Book of Rites*)

The way of heaven is far away; the way of man is near. (*Zuo's Commentary on The Spring and Autumn Annals*)

266

tiānlǐ

天理

Natural Law

The term means the universal law observed by all things in heaven and on earth as well as by human society. Confucian scholars in the Song and Ming dynasties held that the essence of heaven was natural law, and they regarded natural law as the realm of ultimate significance. Natural law is the essence or the source of things, deciding the inherent nature of humans and things. It is the law of nature and the foundation of moral conduct in the human society. Natural law transcends visible, concrete things, but it also exists in each concrete thing. In terms of human nature, natural law expresses itself in the innate good nature one is bestowed upon by heaven, as opposed to "human desire."

CITATIONS

All things are but manifestations of the natural law. (*Writings of the Cheng Brothers*)

Human nature reflects the natural law, which is necessarily benign. (Zhu Xi: *Mencius Variorum*)

267

tiānmìng

天命

Mandate of Heaven

The term means order and bestowment from Heaven. "Mandate of heaven" mainly contains three different meanings: The first is the order of heaven over human affairs. Such order first of all focuses on a change of the supreme ruler's authority: Heaven empowers the virtuous to attack and replace a ruler who has lost his virtue, and thus enjoy the highest and unsurpassed power and benefits. Secondly, mandate of heaven means fate, which is irresistible and imposes limit on human power. Thirdly, the term indicates the natural disposition bestowed by heaven upon human being. According to *The Doctrine of the Mean*, "Mandate of heaven endows one with his nature." Song-dynasty Confucian scholars developed this idea, proposing that human nature was the "nature of mandate of heaven," that is, the inherent pure and good nature one receives from heaven.

CITATIONS

The power and fortune bestowed upon one by heaven are not permanent. (*The Book of Songs*)

That which no man can do but is accomplished is the mandate of heaven. That which no man asks but comes is from fate. (*Mencius*)

268

tiānmìngzhīxìng

天命之性

Character Endowed by Heaven

This term refers to the moral character endowed to a person by Heaven, also known as the "properties of heaven and earth," as opposed to the "properties of *qi*, or vital force." Some early pre-Qin Confucian scholars maintained that human moral characters originated from Heaven. Confucian scholars of the Song Dynasty, inheriting this concept, further propounded the notion of "characters endowed by Heaven," meaning that all people were endowed by Heaven with moral characters. "Characters endowed by Heaven" are purely good, providing the inner basis for a person's moral principle and conduct. However, as human characters are subject to other influences, "characters endowed by Heaven" can be obscured.

CITATIONS

Physical matters take up their shape which acquires the properties of *qi*, or vital force; if we are thus good at returning to it, then the nature endowed by Heaven and Earth will be preserved. (Zhang Zai: *Enlightenment Through Confucian Teachings*)

Characters endowed by Heaven refer to heavenly laws; the way of following those characters refers to human conduct. (*Classified Conversations of Master Zhu Xi*)

269

tiānxià-xīngwáng, pǐfū-yǒuzé
天下兴亡，匹夫有责

The Rise and Fall of All Under Heaven Is the Responsibility of Every Individual.

The view that ordinary people also share responsibility for the fate of the country originated with the famous late Ming- and early Qing-dynasty thinker Gu Yanwu. He stated that the ruler and his officials were in charge of the state apparatus, but guarding all under heaven was the responsibility of every individual, no matter how lowly they may be. In pre-modern China, all under heaven referred to the whole territory of China ruled either directly or nominally by the Son of Heaven. By "state" Gu Yanwu, however, meant something entirely different: the state only refers to one imperial house, while "all under heaven" refers to the whole of the Chinese nation and Chinese civilization. The modern Chinese thinker Liang Qichao built on this idea and put it in more general terms stating that "the rise and fall of all under heaven is the responsibility of every individual," turning it into a clearer and more forceful statement. It was subsequently quoted by so many statesmen and thinkers that it became a household phrase. Ever since, this saying has had tremendous influence in arousing the patriotic spirit among the people of China and making them assume responsibility for the fate of their country.

CITATIONS

When one dynasty is replaced by another, it means the state of the old dynasty perishes. When benevolence and righteousness are obstructed to the point that the powerful lead others to exploit people and people fight each other, it means all under heaven perishes... Safeguarding the state is the concern of rulers, ministers, and officials; while safeguarding all under heaven is the responsibility of every individual, no matter how lowly they may be. (Gu Yanwu: *Record of Daily Study*)

Gu Yanwu said: The rise and fall of all under heaven is the responsibility of every individual, no matter how lowly they may be. (Mai Hua: The Responsibilities of Officials in Charge of Current Border Affairs)

The key to wiping out our country's humiliation lies in our self-renewal... We have a large population, so it is impossible for every individual to achieve such self-renewal. We should do it ourselves whether or not others can also do it. This is just like what Gu Yanwu once said, "The rise and fall of all under heaven is the responsibility of every individual." (Liang Qichao: *Collected Works from the Ice-drinker's Studio*)

270

tóngguī-shūtú
同归殊途

Arrive at the Same Destination via Different Routes / Rely on a Common Ontological Entity

This term means to reach the same goal through different routes. Coming from *The Book of Changes*, the term has two meanings: First, different schools of thought and different people have different understandings of social order and values, and the ways of governance they advocate also vary, but their goals are the same – stability and prosperity of society. Second, though things under heaven manifest themselves in different ways, they all belong or rely on a common ontological entity.

CITATIONS

All people under heaven have the same goal, though they take different routes; they cherish the same concern, but they hold different views. (*The Book of Changes*)

Confucius said, "Under heaven, people have the same goal but they go by different routes." This means that all things under heaven rely on the same ontological entity. (Wang Fuzhi: *Explanatory Notes to The Book of Changes*)

271

wēngù-zhīxīn

温故知新

Review the Old and Learn the New

This term means to review what has been learned and to gain new understanding and new insights. It also means to obtain guidance in the present moment by recalling the past. *Wen* (温) means to review; *gu* (故) means knowledge that has been acquired in the past; *xin* (新) means new and unexplored knowledge. Our predecessors had two main approaches to interpreting this term. According to one approach, reviewing the knowledge acquired in the past and understanding new knowledge should be understood as two actions taking place at the same time. In other words, one gains new knowledge in the course of reviewing the old. According to the other, reviewing the knowledge acquired in the past should be viewed as the basis and precondition for understanding new knowledge. Without reviewing, one would not be able to understand new knowledge. Furthermore, the new knowledge is a development of the old on the basis of rejecting stale and outdated ideas of the past. Today, what this term offers is more than a simple methodology for studying, but rather a fundamental mechanism for the development of an individual, an enterprise, an organization, or even a country. The term expresses a dialectical logic between the old and new, past and present, known and unknown, and inheritance and innovation.

CITATION

Reviewing what you have acquired and learning anew, this way you can be a teacher for others. (*The Analects*)

272

wúyù-zégāng
无欲则刚

People with No Covetous Desires Stand Upright.

People with no covetous desires stand upright and maintain integrity. *Yu* (欲) refers to all sorts of selfish and covetous desires. *Gang* (刚) means fairness, justice, integrity, and forcefulness. *Wuyu* (无欲) does not mean that people should not have any desires, but rather, people should not harbor any selfish or covetous desires. The term tells us a basic principle for people to follow in conducting themselves, and especially for officials in handling office affairs, that is, no temptations should ever sway anyone. One must always conduct oneself properly without seeking to gratify personal interests; one must always seek compliance without seeking fame or wealth; and one must never harbor any greed. This is the way for one to stand upright, firm, and fearless. Like towering cliffs, one may stand tall and indestructible.

CITATIONS

Confucius said, "I have never seen any person of rec titude." Someone responded, "Shen Cheng is such a person." Confucius said, "Shen Cheng has covetous desires too. How can he be of rectitude?" (*The Analects*)

The vast ocean accepts hundreds of rivers emptying into it; people with a broad mind can achieve greatness. Thousands of cliffs stand tall and lofty; people with no covetous desires stand firm and upright. (A couplet composed by Lin Zexu)

273

xiāngfǎn-xiāngchéng

相反相成

Being both Opposite and Complementary

This term refers to two things that are mutually opposite to but complementing each other and that they mutually transform between them. Everything is an antithesis to something else. Both antithetic sides are opposite to each other. Therefore there is mutual exclusion between them, such as *you* and *wu*, long and short, high and low, good and bad, and beautiful and ugly. On the other hand, the nature or the identity of a thing is established due to something antithetic to it. The two opposing sides can transform into each other under certain conditions. This concept emerged in the pre-Qin period. In *The History of the Han Dynasty* written by Ban Gu, the idea was first defined as "two things being both opposite and complementary."

CITATIONS

People all know that ugliness exists as an antithesis of beauty and that evil exists as an antithesis of goodness. Likewise, *you* and *wu* produce each other; what is difficult and what is easy complement each other; long and short exist in contrast, so do high and low; tone and sound are in harmony with each other, and front and back exist because of each other. (*Laozi*)

The relationship between benevolence and righteousness and between respect and harmony is one of mutual opposition and complementation. (*The History of the Han Dynasty*)

274

xiàng

象

Xiang (Semblance)

Xiang (象) refers to a visible but formless image or figure. It approximately has four different meanings. First, it refers to a manifest shape of Dao. Laozi described Dao as "a semblance of the unsubstantial," also called "the great semblance." Second, it indicates a manifest shape of objects. *Xiang* is less concrete or fixed than an object with a shape. It often means celestial phenomena, namely, the movements of the sun, the moon, and the stars, and the occurrence of wind, thunder, clouds, and rain. Celestial phenomena are relative to earthly shapes. Third, it refers to human temperament, namely, the human spirit and mind, manifested in words, deeds, and attitude. Fourth, it refers to figures symbolizing or imitating all things in heaven and on earth. Ancient Chinese created many kinds of systems of *xiang*, through the observation and interpretation of which they elucidated the changes in the movements of nature and of society, and also their laws. Among them, the system of the hexagrams and figures of *The Book of Changes* is the most influential.

CITATIONS

Above, Dao is not manifest, while lower down it is not obscure. It is ceaseless but cannot be described, and it then turns to nothingness. This is called the shape of the shapeless, and the semblance of the unsubstantial. Such a state is called indistinct. (*Laozi*)

In heaven it is semblance, and on earth it has concrete shape, and this demonstrates change of things. (*The Book of Changes*)

Hexagrams and trigrams described in *The Book of Changes* allowed sages to survey the secret of all things under heaven and determine what was fitting through simulation of the shapes of things. That is why they were called semblances. (*The Book of Changes*)

275

xiǎoshuō

小说

Fiction

Fiction is a literary genre primarily concerned with depicting characters to tell a complete story about social life within a setting. Fiction has three main elements, namely, characters, a plot, and a setting. Depending on the length, fiction can be divided into novels, novellas, and short stories. In terms of content, traditional Chinese fiction can be divided into the following broad categories: fantasy stories of gods and spirits, historical fiction, heroic legendary tales, and stories about human relations and social mores. In terms of genre, traditional Chinese fiction is divided into literary sketches, legendary tales, story-tellers' prompt-books, and chapter-based novels. In terms of language, there is fiction in the classical language and vernacular fiction. Traditional Chinese fiction has evolved through different stages, with distinctive features for each period. The myths, legends and historical biographies of the pre-Qin and Han dynasties, and the fables in the works of the earlier Chinese thinkers were the sources of traditional Chinese fiction. The literary sketches by men of letters in the Wei, Jin, Northern and Southern dynasties were embryonic forms of traditional fiction. The legendary tales of the Tang Dynasty marked the eventual emergence of Chinese fiction. The story-tellers' prompt-books in the Song and Yuan dynasties laid the foundation that allowed traditional fiction to reach maturity. The novels of the Ming and Qing dynasties marked the peak in the development of pre-modern fiction. That period is famous for producing four great Chinese classical novels, namely, *Romance of the Three Kingdoms, Journey to the West, Outlaws of the Marsh* and *Dream of the Red Chamber.* During and after the New Culture Movement and the May 4th Movement around 1919, a large amount of modern vernacular fiction appeared, bringing forth a message of science and democracy of the modern age.

CITATIONS

Those writers of stories put together scattered statements. Drawing on what happens around them, they make up parables, writing short pieces. The parts about how to improve one's character and keep good family life are worth reading. (Huan Tan: *New Treatise*)

Fiction is a literary supplement to formal historical accounts. (Xiaohua Zhuren: Foreword to *Strange Tales New and Old*)

276

xiěyì

写意

Freehand Brushwork

Freehand brushwork is one of the traditional methods of brushwork expression in Chinese painting. Using abbreviated and willful brushwork, the artist suggests graphically the meaning and character of the object and its shape. The chief aim is to give rein to the artist's subjective state and mood. It stresses flexibility in brushwork, unrestrained by unimportant details and rejecting naturalistic effects (in contrast with meticulous painting). This style of painting, while seemingly coarse and whimsical, is in fact highly conscious of, and strictly consistent with, standards of artistic creation. Besides demanding close observation and experience of natural objects prior to painting, such as that the various forms within the picture will be laid out appropriately, it also demands solid technical proficiency in order that the artistic intent be formed in imagination before taking shape in painting. Freehand brushwork is divided into greater freehand and lesser freehand, with the former often employing the ink-splashing technique. It had a significant influence on the production of operas and the development of acting techniques in later ages. The freehand style in Chinese-style opera is shown through consciously artificial, stylized motions, accompanied by singing and dancing, to present images artistically on the stage.

CITATIONS

By applying washes without lines, the Buddhist monk Zhongren painted plum blossoms which looked like florid shadows, thus creating a distinctive style of his own. This is what is meant by freehand brushwork! (Xia Wenyan: *The Precious Mirror of Painting*)

People describe paintings of vegetables, fruits, plants, and flowers painted according to the artist's whim, with dots here and there, "freehand brushwork," whereas they see paintings in the detailed style as "naturalistic drawings." (Fang Xun: *On Painting in the Quiet Mountain Studio*)

277

xīnzhī

心知

Mind Cognition

The term means cognitive activities of the mind. As there are different views on the relationship between the mind and the external world, people's understanding of the mind's cognitive process also varies. Some people emphasize the role of the mind in shaping ethical standards in daily life and making them a source of inner strength. Cognition of the mind is a prerequisite for moral cultivation and ethical living. As the mind is often in a blocked or unstable state, it needs to be nurtured with proper guidance before it can play its due role. However, others argue that the mind's cognitive activities make one concerned about the evolving complexity of the external world and feel anxious about life. It is therefore necessary to get rid of the mind's cognitive activities so as to leave the mind in a state of tranquility free from outside interference.

CITATION

How can people appreciate Dao? The answer is to use one's mind. How can the mind know? The answer is concentration of the mind in tranquility. (*Xunzi*)

278

xíngxiān-zhīhòu

行先知后

First Action, Then Knowledge

The term represents one interpretation of the relationship between "knowledge" and "action." Regarding the relationship between "knowledge" and "action," Wang Fuzhi and others argued that "action precedes knowledge." Wang acknowledged that an understanding of the principles underlying human relations in everyday life is interrelated with the application of these principles, but in terms of sequence, only through "action" can one obtain "knowledge." "Action" is the source of "knowledge" and has a decisive impact on "knowledge." If one can "act," one inevitably "knows" about one's actions, but the ability to "know" does not necessarily translate into the ability to "act."

CITATION

Only after acting can one know the difficulties involved; without efforts to act one cannot know. (Wang Fuzhi: *Explicating the Lessons of the Four Books*)

279

xuán

玄

Xuan (Mystery)

The term first described the original state of everything, which is profound and mysterious. Laozi used it to describe Dao and virtue as being in a profound and mysterious state, calling Dao "a mystery within a mystery," or "virtue of mystery." Ancient Chinese thinkers like Yang Xiong and Ge Hong went a step further, describing *xuan* (玄) as being the supreme original source or the primal ontological existence of all things in heaven and on earth. In this sense *xuan* is a kind of absolute existence, formless and imageless, which transcends all concrete things. Later on, *xuanxue* (玄学), or learning of the mystery, developed, referring to the quest into the original source or ontological existence of the world.

CITATIONS

You and *wu* are from the same origin but have different names. They are all extremely mysterious and profound and lead to all changes. (Yang Xiong: *Supreme Mystery*)

Xuan is the origin of nature and the source of all things. (Ge Hong: *Baopuzi*)

280

xuèqì

血气

Vitality / Vital Force

The term refers to vitality which is needed for the human or animal body to sustain its life and which reflects the state of life. It is something one is born with, representing the body's needs of material things. A person exhibits different levels of vitality at different stages of life, reflecting changes in the strength of life. Vitality is unstable in youth; it reaches its peak in the prime of life, and in old age it wanes. Furthermore, different people have different levels of vitality, some overflowing with vigor, while others are subdued. People's vitality can be changed by means of rites, music and through education; it is the basis for shaping a person's moral and emotional trait.

CITATIONS

Confucius said, "One should guard against three things in life. In his youth his vital force is unstable and he should guard against lust. As his vital force strengthens in the prime of life, he should guard against aggressive behavior. In his old age his vital force weakens, and he should guard against greed." (*The Analects*)

All things born between heaven and earth with vital force have consciousness; and with consciousness they all love their own kind. (*Xunzi*)

281

xúnmíng-zéshí

循名责实

Hold Actualities According to Its Name

An actual object should be assessed according to the name referring to it. Holding actualities according to its name was an important means for ancient Chinese to govern the state. In actual human relations concerning ethics and morality, every specific role or status had its name, which determined the character or responsibilities of that status. People with certain status had to be assessed on the basis of their status, and it was required that their actual words and actions corresponded to the character and responsibilities determined by the name of their status.

CITATIONS

The way of governance is to bestow office according to responsibilities, who was required to carry out duties as was required by the name (i.e. the office), to exercise power over life and death, and examine and weigh officials with outstanding capabilities. (*Hanfeizi*)

To assess the actual thing or substance according to its name means to demand an actual standard. To determine the name of a thing or substance according to actualities is the standard for naming the name. (*Dengxizi*)

282

yǎyuè

雅乐

Fine Music

The term refers to a kind of classical music in China. Noble and pure, it was the music used by kings in ancient times when worshipping heaven, earth, and ancestors, receiving congratulations from other quarters of the world, or holding feasts and major ceremonial activities. Chinese classical music often eulogized the royal court's accomplishments; its melodies were tranquil and stately, its wording elegant and tasteful, and its performance of song and dance followed explicit codes of etiquette. Rulers of all dynasties used this kind of music as an effective means to instruct their people and promote civic virtue. As a courtly tradition, the music was necessarily conservative. However, throughout history the assimilation of elements of folk song and dance, as well as the music and dance of foreign lands, inevitably led to innovation. Thus, it maintained throughout the ages the highest levels of musical excellence. After the Tang Dynasty, this kind of music spread to other Asian countries such as Japan, Korea, and Vietnam, becoming a constituent part of their musical culture.

CITATIONS

Confucius said, "I detest replacing red with purple and interfering refined classical music with the music of the State of Zheng. I loathe those who overthrow the state with their glib tongues." (*The Analects*)

At the time, Liu De, Prince Xian of Hejian, was an exceptionally talented man, and he believed that music and ceremony were essential to the proper governing of the state. As a result he donated all the documents of classical music he had collected to the court. (*The History of the Han Dynasty*)

Xun Xu had a sensitive ear for musical tones. Some, recognizing his musical gift, recommended him for a position overseeing musical rules and revising classical music. (Liu Yiqing: *A New Account of Tales of the World*)

283

yánbùjìnyì
言不尽意

Words Cannot Fully Express Thought.

Words cannot fully express the fundamental understanding of the world. According to *The Book of Changes*, words are inadequate for expressing what one means and that was why the hexagram images were made to convey the ideas of the sages. Xun Can, Wang Bi, and other metaphysicians of the Wei and Jin dynasties further elucidated this concept. Their understanding of the relationship between language and thinking was determined by their understanding of the ontological existence or original source of the world. They believed that the world's ontological existence or original source was *wu* (无), which was beyond anything tangible. *Wu* had no specific form or attribute, and it was therefore impossible to name or describe it. Thus, language was found to have its limitations in expressing thought.

CITATIONS

Written characters cannot fully express what the author wants to say, nor can words fully express his thought and knowledge. (*The Book of Changes*)

The notions beyond the images and the words beyond the "appended phrases" are deeply stored in them, and so they cannot be expressed. (Pei Songzhi: *Annotations on The History of the Three Kingdoms*)

284

yánjìnyì
言尽意

Words Can Fully Express Thought.

Words can fully express the fundamental understanding of the universe. The relationship between language and thought was a prominent topic of debate in the Wei and Jin dynasties. Ouyang Jian did not accept the view of Xun Can and Wang Bi, who alleged that "words cannot fully express thought." Instead, he put forward the notion that "words can fully express thought." In his opinion, thought represents perceptions of objects and reason, while names and words are reflections of them and are determined by things and reason. As a thought is acquired and expressed, it is analyzed and realized by names and words. Thoughts and their correspondent words are accord with each other and inseparable. Thus thought can be fully and exhaustively expressed.

CITATION

Names change when the objects they refer to change. Language changes on the basis of reason. That is like the echo responding to a sound or a shadow following a shape. They are not to be considered as separate things. If they are not separate things, then there is nothing that cannot be fully expressed. Therefore, I believe language can fully express thought. (Ouyang Jian: *On Fully Expressing Ideas*)

285

Yán-Huáng
炎黄

The Fiery Emperor and the Yellow Emperor / Emperor Yan and Emperor Huang

Emperor Yan (the Fiery Emperor) and Emperor Huang (the Yellow Emperor), legendary Chinese rulers in pre-dynastic times, were actually tribal leaders. Emperor Yan, whose family name was Jiang, was known as Shennongshi while Emperor Huang, whose family name was Gongsun, was known as Xuanyuanshi. They originally lived in central China where their tribes gradually merged with those in eastern and southern China. People in these tribes proliferated and made up the main body of the Chinese nation (who were referred to as the Han people after the Han Dynasty and Tang people after the Tang Dynasty). Hence, they have been revered as the ancestors of the Chinese nation. Their tribes, and the tribe headed by the Yellow Emperor in particular, achieved the highest level of civilization. Many important cultural advancements and technical innovations in ancient China were believed to be created by these two tribes. They have therefore been seen as the forefathers of the Chinese civilization. In modern times, they have been considered as symbols of the Chinese nation and Chinese culture. Today, Chinese descendants residing in different parts of the world proudly regard themselves as "descendants of the Fiery Emperor and the Yellow Emperor" or simply "descendants of the Yellow Emperor." In this regard, "Yan and Huang" have become cultural symbols of the Chinese nation.

CITATIONS

With the collapse of the ruling order of Emperor of the Zhou Dynasty, by the end of the Spring and Autumn Period, various vassal states had been defeated, but numerous descendants of Emperors Yan, Huang, Yao, and Shun remained. (*The History of the Han Dynasty*)

We, descendants of the Fiery Emperor and the Yellow Emperor, have devoted ourselves to the revolution. ("To All Officers and Soldiers Fighting the War of Resistance Against Japanese Aggression" issued by the then national government of China)

286

yīwù-liǎngtǐ

一物两体

One Thing in Two Fundamental States

Qi (气), or vital force, consists of two opposing aspects. According to the Song-dynasty philosopher Zhang Zai, everything in the world consists of *qi*. On the one hand, *qi* is a whole and one thing; on the other, it consists of pairs of contradictory states, such as the real and the unreal, motion and stillness, concentration and diffusion, and clarity and opacity. Without interaction between the opposite states, the whole cannot exist. Likewise, without the whole, there can be no interaction between the opposite states. Contradictions within the whole constitute the source of changes of *qi* and all things made of *qi*.

CITATION

One thing with two states, that is *qi*, or vital force. As one whole thing, *qi* has miraculous movements, caused by interaction between the two opposites; and such movements create endless changes. This is why heaven has three aspects (the whole and the two states). (Zhang Zai: *Enlightenment Through Confucian Teachings*)

287

yǐwú-wéiběn
以无为本

Wu Is the Origin.

Wu (无) is regarded as the original source or ontological existence of the world in classical Chinese thinking. Laozi claimed that "*you* (有) is born out of *wu*." This concept was further developed by He Yan, Wang Bi, and other thinkers of the Wei and Jin dynasties, who maintained that heaven, earth, and all things in the world originate from *wu*. No specific being, they argued, can be the original source or ontological existence of another being, much less of the world. The formation and existence of everything depend on *wu*, which is the fundamental source that transcends all tangible beings. Only an intangible and unidentifiable ontological existence gives countless specific beings their functions.

CITATION

All things under heaven exist by means of *you*. The formation and existence of *you* originate from *wu*. To maintain *you* we must return to *wu*. (Wang Bi: *Annotations on Laozi*)

288

yǐzhí-bàoyuàn

以直报怨

Repaying a Grudge with Rectitude

Treat a person you hold a grudge against with upright behavior. "Repaying a grudge with rectitude" was a principle proposed by Confucius for dealing with grudges. He felt that both "repaying a grudge with a grudge" and "repaying a grudge with kindness" were incorrect. Confucius argued that one should not deliberately seek vengeance out of momentary anger, nor should one conceal resentment over a grudge and repay it with kindness. Rather, one should analyze the rights and wrongs of the episode which created the grudge, and respond according to the principles of rectitude.

CITATION

Someone asked, "How about repaying a grudge with kindness?" Confucius said, "Then how would you repay kindness? Repay a grudge with rectitude, and repay kindness with kindness." (*The Analects*)

289

yǒuróng-nǎidà
有容乃大

A Broad Mind Achieves Greatness.

A broad mind achieves greatness. *Yourong* (有容) means that one has the capacity to accommodate others. *Da* (大) refers to great courage and an important cause. *Yourong* is a moral standard, and more importantly, contains wisdom for survival. It is a conscious act of morality in pursuit of social harmony by managing and regulating relations between oneself and others on the basis of recognizing and respecting individual and social differences, without resorting to deliberate self-abnegation or making unprincipled compromise. The term teaches people how to conduct themselves, particularly officials in exercising their administrative powers. That is, they should have a broad mind, open to different views and different things, like the sea accepting numerous rivers flowing into it. This is the way to cultivate great character and important achievements. Its meaning is similar to the term *houde-zaiwu* (厚德载物 have ample virtue and carry all things).

CITATIONS

Tolerance and patience lead people to success, and broadmindedness to merits and virtues. (*The Book of History*)

The vast ocean accepts hundreds of rivers emptying into it; people with a broad mind can achieve greatness. Thousands of cliffs stand tall and lofty; people with no covetous desires stand firm and upright. (A couplet composed by Lin Zexu)

290

yǔmín-gēngshǐ

与民更始

Make a Fresh Start with the People

The term means to make political reform together with the people. *Gengshi* (更始) means to make a fresh start. The term used to refer to a new emperor ascending the throne, taking a new reign title or implementing a series of new policies. Later, it came to mean that the rulers worked together with the people trying to change the status quo and opening up new prospects. The term reflects a profound and far-reaching thought of putting people first, and highlights the spirit of monarchs and the people working with one heart and one mind to abolish what is old and establish in its place a new order.

CITATION

I praise ancient emperors Yao and Shun; I like the Shang and Zhou dynasties. I have issued an imperial decree to either exempt criminals from punishment or commute their sentences on the basis of the old practice and new rules, so that we may open up a new era together with the people. (*The History of the Han Dynasty*)

291

zàizhōu-fùzhōu
载舟覆舟

Carry or Overturn the Boat / Make or Break

Water can carry a boat, but can also overturn it. Here, water is compared to the people, while the boat is compared to the ruler. The phrase, "carry or overturn the boat," reveals the importance of popular support: people are the critical force that decides the future of a regime and a country. This is consistent with such political doctrines as "the people are the foundation of the state," and "it is necessary to follow the mandate of heaven and comply with people's wishes." Since ancient times, this term has served as a warning to the ruler, reminding him of the need to respect local conditions and popular will, to govern the country for the people, and to anticipate dangers in times of security.

CITATION

The ruler is the boat and the people are the water. Water can carry the boat but can also overturn it. This is the very truth. (*Xunzi*)

292

zhèngmíng

正名

Rectification of Names

This refers to the rectification of what things are called so that name and reality correspond. A name is what is used to refer to a thing, which determines the attributes of the thing and its relations with other things. "Reality" refers to a thing or an entity that its name refers to. The name of a thing should conform to what the thing actually is. However, very often name and reality do not match in real life. To deal with this situation, the name of a thing should not go beyond the nature of the thing; likewise, the reality referred to by the name must not go beyond the scope that the name implies. The "rectification of names" is an important way to maintain the social order constructed by the names. Various schools of thoughts have agreed on the necessity of rectifying names, but they differ in their views of the concrete meanings of the names to be rectified.

CITATIONS

If names are not rectified, one's argument will not be proper. If speech is not proper, nothing can be accomplished. If nothing is accomplished, rites and music will not flourish. If rites and music do not flourish, punishments will not be meted out properly. If punishments are not meted out properly, people will have no guidance as how to behave. (*The Analects*)

Rectification is to bring forth what actuality is. To bring forth what actuality is is what it means to rectify the name. (*Gongsun Long's Papers*)

293

zhèngxīn

正心

Rectify One's Heart / Mind

This term means to rectify our mind so as to follow moral principles in daily life. Rectifying one's heart or mind is one of the eight notions from the philosophical text *The Great Learning*, the other seven being "studying things," "acquiring knowledge," "being sincere in thought," "cultivating oneself," "regulating one's family well," "governing the state properly," and "bringing peace to all under heaven." These constitute important stages in the moral cultivation advocated by the Confucian school. "Rectifying one's mind" has as its preceding stage "being sincere in thought." In the course of following the moral principles earnestly in daily life, people are inevitably influenced by sentiments such as anger, fear, joy, and worries, which will, to some degree, lead a person astray. Therefore, one must always try to rectify one's mind and avoid being swayed by any interference, so as to keep to the observance of moral principles in daily life.

CITATIONS

When thought has been made sincere but the mind is perhaps still somewhat biased, then it is not possible for a person to stay pure and unbiased. Therefore one should make efforts to rectify one's mind. (*Classified Conversations of Master Zhu Xi*)

To rectify one's mind means to cultivate one's good conscience without the least conjecture, arbitrariness, stubbornness, or egoism. (*Records of Great Learning*)

294

zhèng zhě zhèng yě

政者正也

Governance Means Rectitude.

Zheng (政), or governance, refers to policy and managing the country, while *zheng* (正), or rectitude, refers to adherence to principle, decent behavior, and handling matters with fairness. This term has two meanings. First, it emphasizes that those who govern should adhere to principle, behave correctly, and handle matters with fairness. Second, it emphasizes that at a moral level, those who govern should be strict with themselves, that they should play an exemplary role and thus show their subordinates and the people how to follow the right path and comply with social norms. It is a concrete expression of the idea "rule by man" and "governing by virtue" in ancient times.

CITATIONS

When asked by Ji Kang about governance, Confucius replied, "Governance is all about rectitude. If you lead along the right path, who would dare not to follow you?" (*The Analects*)

Confucius said, "When a ruler acts in the right way, things get done even without him giving any order. When he is not right, people will not comply even when ordered." (*The Analects*)

295

zhī chǐ ér hòu yǒng

知耻而后勇

Having a Feeling of Shame Gives Rise to Courage.

The notion that having a feeling of shame gives rise to courage comes from the saying that "to have a feeling of shame is to be near to having courage." Having a feeling of shame means to be ashamed of one's own mistakes as well as to hate the misbehavior of others. Mencius believed this to be one of the basic things humans must do. In Confucian thought courage is one of three universal virtues along with wisdom and love for others. Linking shame and courage was meant to impel people to face their shortcomings squarely and work hard for improvement and perfection. The concept embodies the spirit of individuals, companies, organizations, ethnic groups, and the whole nation in achieving self-respect, self-motivation, and self-improvement.

CITATIONS

Wisdom, love for others, and courage, these three are the universal virtues of all under heaven. (*The Book of Rites*)

To love learning is to be near to wisdom, to practice with vigor is to be near to love for others, and to have a feeling of shame is to be near to courage. (*The Book of Rites*)

296

zhīxíng-héyī

知行合一

Unity of Knowledge and Action

This is one interpretation of the relationship between "knowledge" and "action." Based on the concept in philosophy of the mind that "there are no *li* (理), or principles, outside the mind," Wang Shouren made the argument that "there is unity of knowledge and action." He felt that it was impossible to separate an understanding of the principles underlying human relations in everyday life from the application of these principles, that these were two sides of the same thing. If there was "knowledge" in the mind, it would surely be put into practice, as "action" was the natural use of "knowledge." If it was not applied, it could not be true "knowledge." On the other hand, "action" would also bring about deeper knowledge. Without "knowledge," mere unconscious or forced behavior would not constitute proper "action."

CITATIONS

Searching for principles outside the mind is the reason why people separate knowledge from action; searching for principles within one's mind is how sages teach about the unity of knowledge and action. (*Records of Great Learning*)

When knowledge is genuine and substantive, it becomes action; when actions bring about self-awareness and keen perceptions, they become knowledge. "Knowledge" and "action" were indivisible to begin with, and it was only because scholars later treated them as two separate things, contrary to their original nature, that there was a theory of their being united and developing together. (*Records of Great Learning*)

297

zhīxiān-xínghòu

知先行后

First Knowledge, Then Action

The term represents one interpretation of the relationship between "knowledge" and "action." Regarding the relationship between "knowledge" and "action," scholars like Cheng Yi and Zhu Xi argued that "knowledge precedes action." They did not deny that an understanding of the principles underlying human relations in everyday life is interrelated with the application of these principles, nor did they feel that either of the two should be overlooked. However, in terms of sequence, they argued that "knowledge" came first, that it was the basis of "action," and that "action" took place through the guidance of "knowledge." Only by first understanding the principles underlying human relations in everyday life can we make our words and deeds follow the rules which govern human activities.

CITATIONS

Knowledge must be present before it can be acted upon, just as light must illuminate the path to be followed. (*Writings of the Cheng Brothers*)

Knowledge and action are interdependent, just as eyes cannot walk without the feet, and feet cannot see without the eyes. In terms of sequence, knowledge comes first; in terms of importance, action is more important. (*Classified Conversations of Master Zhu Xi*)

298

zhí

直

Rectitude

The basic meaning of "rectitude" is uprightness. More specifically, there are two interpretations of "rectitude." The first interpretation refers to words and deeds that meet the moral standards or the rules of propriety. To be "upright" is to refrain from doing anything immoral or illegal for the sake of personal gain. However, because there are different understandings of morality and propriety, there are also different views, even conflicting ones, of how "rectitude" is manifested. The second interpretation of being "upright" is acting in accordance with facts and not concealing the truth in order to meet the expectations or needs of others.

CITATIONS

Confucius asked, "Who said Weisheng Gao is upright? Someone asked him for vinegar, and (without saying he did not have any) he got some from his neighbor for the man." (*The Analects*)

Duke Ai of the State of Lu asked, "How can I win over the people?" Confucius replied, "If you promote upright people and put them above crooked ones, you will win over the people; if you promote crooked people and put them above upright ones, you will not win over the people." (*The Analects*)

299

zhì dà guó ruò pēng xiǎo xiān
治大国若烹小鲜

Governing a Big Country Is Like Cooking Small Fish.

Governing a big country is like cooking small fish. This is a fundamental principle of state governance based on the concept of "non-action" advocated by Laozi. When cooking small fish, one needs to mix various kinds of ingredients, carefully control time of cooking and degree of heating, so that every small fish is equally tasty. One should not stir the fish too much in cooking so that they will not fall apart into small pieces. Similarly, as a big country has a vast territory, a large population, and wide differences among regions and social groups, those who govern the land must be meticulous and thoughtful and take all factors into consideration, so that their policies and measures benefit everyone. Once fundamental policies for governance are adopted, those who govern should not intervene excessively in social activities.

CITATION

Governing a big country is like cooking small fish. When the country is ruled by Dao, demons can neither disrupt it nor harm the people. Even sages acting in Dao principles will not bring harm to people either. Free from harms by demons and sages, people stand to gain all benefits. (*Laozi*)

300

zhōng

忠

Loyalty

Loyalty involves doing one's utmost. A person in a certain position or office should wholeheartedly perform his duties and must not be influenced by personal interests. The object of loyalty can be the person who appoints you to your post or grants you a position; it can also be an organization, group or the state where you belong. For example, in ancient society it was thought the monarch should be loyal to the people while the subjects should be loyal to the monarch.

CITATIONS

Zengzi said, "Each day I reflect on myself several times. Have I failed to be loyal to someone when offering my advice to him? Have I failed to keep my word to my friends? Have I failed to review the teachings I have learned?" (*The Analects*)

To do all one can is what loyalty requires. (Zhu Xi: *The Analects Variorum*)